THE
ATTACKER'S
ADVANTAGE

THE
ATTACKER'S
ADVANTAGE

Turning Uncertainty into
Breakthrough Opportunities

RAM CHARAN

PUBLICAFFAIRS
New York

PublicAffairs books are available at special discounts for bulk purchases in the
U.S. by corporations, institutions, and other organizations. For more information,
please contact the Special Markets Department at the Perseus Books Group, 2300
Chestnut Street, Suite 200, Philadelphia, PA 19103, call (800) 810-4145, ext. 5000,
or e-mail special.markets@perseusbooks.com.

Library of Congress Cataloging-in-Publication Data
Charan, Ram.
    The attacker's advantage : turning uncertainty into breakthrough opportunities
/ Ram Charan.
      pages   cm
    Includes bibliographical references and index.
    ISBN 978-1-61039-474-1 (hardback) — ISBN 978-1-61039-475-8 (e-book) —
978-1-61039-568-7 (International)
    1. Uncertainty. 2. Strategic planning. 3. Organizational change. I. Title.

HB615.C583 2015
658.4'012--dc23

                                                                        2014035570
First Edition

10 9 8 7 6 5 4 3 2 1

Dedicated to the hearts and souls
of the joint family of twelve siblings and cousins
living under one roof for fifty years,
whose personal sacrifices
made my formal education possible.

CONTENTS

||||||||||||||||||||||||||||||||||||||||||||||||||||||||||||||||||||||||||||||||||||||||||||||||||||||||||||||||||||||||||||||||||||||||||||||||||||||||||||||

WHAT IS THE ATTACKER'S ADVANTAGE?

WE FEEL UNCERTAINTY in our bones: competitors that appear in an instant and scale up almost as quickly, the algorithmic revolution, a growing pool of economic contenders from virtually every part of the world, a global financial system that will not be reformed. These are just a few of the many forces that can permanently alter moneymaking for a company, industry, or entire economic sector and make uncertainty the fundamental leadership challenge of our time. The question we all ask is: "How can I make decisions and lead when things change so unpredictably and fast?"

In this book I explain the capabilities you need to succeed in this new era of frequent sharp bends in the road. The attacker's advantage is the perceptual acuity to detect ahead of others forces that could radically reshape a market space so that you can position your business to make the next move first. It is the mind-set to overcome fear of uncertainty and find the opportunities in it and the courage to move forward despite the unknowns. It is the ability to gain the advantage with speed, with focus, and without breaking morale.

By pinpointing the sources of uncertainty, defining a path forward, and making the necessary frequent adjustments to steer your organization along it, you will see that uncertainty is not something to fear. On the contrary, by immersing yourself in it you can discover possibilities for creating something new and immensely valuable. The more you embrace uncertainty and practice the skills to deal with it, the more self-confidence you will develop and the better prepared you will be to lead.

PART I

THE FUNDAMENTAL LEADERSHIP
CHALLENGE OF OUR TIME

CHAPTER 1

Bends in the Road

TAKING CONTROL OF uncertainty is the fundamental leadership challenge of our time.

This is not a hypothesis extrapolated from arm's-length research. It emerges from what I have learned in working as an advisor with hundreds of business leaders, ranging from board members to business unit managers, in scores of companies and multiple industries around the world. I have had close relationships with many of them over the course of several decades. These relationships have enabled me to track actions and decisions as they unfold. I talk regularly with hundreds of other leaders, always asking questions and exchanging information. Against this backdrop of experience, I can say with confidence that the immense uncertainty I see today's business leaders facing is something truly unique. In its scale, its speed, the ferocity of its impact, and its increasing ubiquity, it is qualitatively different—by orders of magnitude—from anything that has gone before.

We all know that life is full of uncertainties, of course. Most of those that businesses face are familiar. Some are operational, such as optimizing production for shifts in demand, launching a new product, or adjusting to changing interest rates. Others are career uncertainties that can affect your job security or future opportunities, such as bad decisions made by bosses who favor less competent rivals. Some are macro: geopolitical conflict (on the upswing these days), climate change, and a seriously unstable global financial system.

What's new is structural uncertainty. It is structural because the forces now at work can explode the existing structure of your market space or your industry, putting it at risk of being drastically diminished or completely eliminated. These forces are long term and irresistible. For those who are unprepared, the massive changes they bring are sudden bends in the road that appear seemingly without warning to obscure whatever future you envisioned for your business. But in a world economy projected to grow a net $30 trillion in the coming decade, human needs and wants are always changing. The opportunities are boundless for those who can anticipate and take control of them to create new businesses, new business models, new market segments, and even new industries.

Structural uncertainty is global and yet at the same time atomistic. A growing army of change creators everywhere is empowered by the Internet and low-cost wireless communication. In theory there are potentially seven billion of them: the entire population of the world. One could be Amol Bhave, a seventeen-year-old from Jabalpur, India, who is among the more than 800,000 people around the world who have signed up with the online educational venture edX, jointly sponsored by MIT and Harvard. In March 2013 he learned that he had been accepted at MIT after scoring 97 percent on edX's circuits and electronics course. He told the *Financial Times*: "It opened doors to me for getting into colleges such as MIT which I could never even have dreamt of getting into from my town."[1]

Every day more of the seven billion have instant access to any and all knowledge and insights that exist, as well as the ability to collaborate with others as never before. Their ideas can be scaled up swiftly, because capital is readily available to fund promising ideas. For digital companies, the scaling can be accomplished extremely fast and at low incremental cost. On the other side of the coin, consumers have acquired great new powers because of digitization and online connectivity—including social media, reviews, and instant price comparisons—that give them information and options they never had before. Their preferences can shift en masse, even globally, destroying or diminishing whole industries and creating new ones—adding yet another dimension to the uncertainty. Finally, every uncertainty is magnified by quantum increases in the speed of change, largely brought about by the revolutions in computer and communications technologies.

The Essentials for Leading in Uncertainty

Steering your business through structural uncertainty will call for a distinctly different type of leadership than the one you were trained for and are likely currently exercising, requiring a radically different mind-set and new skills for anticipating events and going on the attack.

The advantage now goes to those who create change, not just learn to live with it. Instead of waiting and reacting, such leaders immerse themselves in the ambiguities of the external environment, sort through them before things are settled and known, set a path, and steer their organization decisively onto it. They conceive of a new need or a total redefinition of an existing need, often with a new business model in mind. They paint a specific picture of what the new company will be. Then they take the organization, along with its external constituencies, on the offensive.

No matter how successful it has made you, your past experience won't ensure success in this new world. Most leaders moving up in an organization have received feedback and been rewarded for such characteristics as being a great communicator and motivator of people, having vision, being decisive, and above all else, delivering the numbers Wall Street wants. Most of the 360-degree evaluations companies use focus on essentially the same traits. I have yet to see one that includes those qualities that I believe are now crucial for meeting the fundamental leadership challenge of our time: perceiving the sources of uncertainty ahead of others, taking advantage of uncertainty to go on the offense, and preparing and steering the organization to adapt in tune with sudden changes in the environment.

Many leaders wait for uncertainties in the external environment to firm up before they react to them. With blind faith in the core competencies and momentum of their established companies, the deniers focus on the most immediate symptoms of shrinking margins and market share and fight back as they always have, typically by lowering prices, increasing promotions, cutting costs deeply, and improving service. Their rationalizations are reinforced by short-term but temporary success, holding Wall Street and its obsolescent metrics at bay (more about these metrics later).

Given the realities of the changes taking place now, these behaviors are rearview mirror thinking. Even if your company focuses on other skills and attributes, you should make it your personal challenge to prepare yourself to lead in the face of structural uncertainty.

From the time I first recognized the immensity of the changes under way today, I have worked to develop practical ways for business leaders to not just defend against them but instead take advantage of them. What I have found is that those who are best prepared to lead now and in the future in this era of big bends in the road have the following skills and abilities:

1. Perceptual acuity
2. A mind-set to see opportunity in uncertainty
3. The ability to see a new path forward and commit to it
4. Adeptness in managing the transition to the new path
5. Skill in making the organization steerable and agile

The remainder of this book explains each of these fully, gives you the tools and insights to develop them, and shows you how others have put them into practice.

Perceptual acuity. Have the psychological and mental preparedness to "see around corners" and spot potentially significant anomalies, contradictions, and oddities in the external landscape ahead of others. Some people are born with it, but it can be learned and even institutionalized. You can sharpen whatever skill you have if you continuously practice being on the alert, sensing the signals of change, and looking for the message in them. You can improve your acuity and cross-check your personal psychological biases by triangulating your perceptions with a diverse group of leaders and experts on a disciplined, regular basis. That will also widen the lens through which you see the world. Develop the habit of detecting sources of uncertainty, including the catalysts—the human beings who drive it—particularly those outside of your industry, and do the mental exercise of thinking through the potential implications. Searching for what is new and reflecting on what it could mean will help you see your business in a different light and spark ideas for new growth trajectories. You will need to expand your networks, relationships, and sources of information far beyond your company and industry, to include governments, nongovernmental organizations (NGOs), and ecosystem partners.

A mind-set to see opportunity in uncertainty. Recognize that uncertainty is an invitation to go on the attack and be ready to take your organization to a new place in the changing landscape. Unless you are caught by surprise and are totally short of time, you should never be on the defensive. Be intellectually honest when you sense a structural break, and accept reality when the core competencies that made your organization successful are no longer valuable or are potentially a hindrance to going in a more promising direction. Every journey encounters obstacles, but some are psychological and prevent you from getting off the ground. A keen awareness of your particular blockages will help you overcome them.

The ability to see a new path forward and commit to it. You have to be willing to build whatever new capabilities you will need, which will include a high level of proficiency in the use of digitization and algorithms. As you search for opportunities and crystallize a new game and a new money-making model, focus on the end-to-end consumer experience and imagine how external changes and digitization can allow you to create a new and compelling one. Pursue it with tenacity. Identify the obstacles you need to overcome and the blockages that stand in your way and attack them. Engage with your bosses and top team (and board of directors, if you are a chief executive officer) so they come around and see the same realities of the external environment. Don't expect everyone to agree with your view of where to take the business, but have the courage of your convictions. Build a bridge of information with people in government to understand their views and help them learn about the structural uncertainties affecting your industry and its consumers.

Adeptness in managing the transition to the new path. Going on the attack may require a major shift as well as constant adjustment in setting priorities and ensuring financial health, particularly when it comes to cash. Stay connected to both external and internal realities to know when to accelerate and when to shift the short-term/long-term balance, with a sharp eye on cash flow and debt. You can win credibility with investors by creating and meeting milestones for the steps the organization will take in the near term to build the company's future. You also have to seek and court investors who understand what you're doing and will make the journey with you.

Skill in making the organization steerable and agile. You cannot succeed unless you bring the organization along with you in whatever new direction you take. Learn to make it agile, or steerable, by linking the external realities in real time to people assignments, priorities, decision-making power, budgeting and capital allocation, and key performance indicators (KPIs). The most powerful tool for achieving these goals is the "joint practice session" (JPS), in which leaders from across a company simultaneously share information, make decisions, integrate actions, and follow through. One major characteristic of the JPS is resolving the conflicts that are endemic to any organization. Another is redirecting resources and movements of people speedily in tune with changes in the external environment.

Get Ready for Discomfort

Taking advantage of the landscape that is emerging will almost certainly call for significant changes in how you define your business. Indeed, in many cases it will mean starting a new and different business that could sooner or later eclipse your biggest revenue maker or cash generator. Either of these courses is essentially an entrepreneurial act on a grand scale, one that leaders in legacy companies have little experience with. The risks make them uncomfortable, so they stall. They ignore the risk of *not* going into a new game and sticking too long with a business that is ripe for transformation, often through some form of digitization (remember, for example, Blockbuster, Kodak, and Borders).

India-based "Excelo" illustrates the sort of scenario you might face. It grew from an information technology outsourcing company to a powerhouse in helping companies redesign their IT processes to reduce cost, cut cycle time, and improve productivity. The dominant logic of its business has been labor arbitrage—that is, much lower labor costs than if the client company did the work in-house. It had long-standing ties with the IT shops of its customers and had superb expertise in their respective industries. But the CEO, who had had deep relationships with client companies throughout his career, noticed that a change was brewing. Customers were seeking help in using mathematics-based software solutions to radically change their businesses. Meeting that need would mean shifting Excelo's focus and acquiring new expertise. Its core business was still making money, although margins were being squeezed by intense competition. Should the company make this shift? If so, it had to move fast before other companies jumped in. But that would mean hiring lots of people with new expertise, and sooner or later, letting many others go, including dedicated middle managers who had built the business but whose expertise was now obsolete. The head of Excelo now had uncomfortable decisions to make. Since the new trajectory would claim a growing share of the company's financial resources, spending on the existing business must be cut back. By how much? How fast? Could the transition destroy the company's heart and soul? How would the media react when so many good people were let go?

Such uncomfortable decisions are part of the new game. Senior leaders and boards at a growing number of companies are now wrestling with similar issues. The pressure affects middle managers, too; at the profit-and-loss (P&L) business unit level, the unnerving question is whether senior people will allow you to have lower earnings in the short run to pursue more promising opportunities. They face the formidable challenge of persuading their bosses to change their priorities.

Not every new trajectory will involve such dire issues, but the greatest risk of all is that leaders who face the need for radical change will deliberate too long and discover that the world has passed them by. At the right moment, you need the inner strength and conviction to take a leap when the outcome is uncertain. You have to move the organization at the right speed, with the right people, which means constantly adjusting it to steer through bends and twists.

—

HOW YOU DEAL with uncertainty as you move ahead puts you in one of two worlds. The first is the legacy world of core competencies, incremental gains, and defensiveness. The second is the one you have to be in if you want to be an attacker: the world of large-scale entrepreneurs who create a new need, scale it up quickly, and put a bend in the road for the traditional players.

CHAPTER 2

Why Structural Uncertainty Is Different

WHEN I WAS growing up in India, my family ran a shoe shop in a town of 100,000 people forty miles north of Delhi. It was surrounded by farmland. Our customers were farmers, most of whom made a simple living. When the yearly monsoon came the farmers mainly stayed home. That was our dry spell: we sold very few pairs of shoes. We never knew exactly when the rain would start, how long it would last, or how heavy it would be—but we knew it would come, and we prepared for the dip in sales and potential cash shortage by reducing our inventory ahead of time. The precise timing of the monsoon was an operational uncertainty that we recognized and learned to manage around.

Now imagine that one day a construction crew arrives in my town and begins to lay the concrete and weld the steel that will soon become a superstore. This would be a structural uncertainty, and if we didn't see it ahead of time, we would be out of business. The precise end of the monsoon doesn't matter much when you're being blown away by a structural uncertainty like this one.

You can manage an operational uncertainty with existing tools. But a structural uncertainty arises from your external environment. It is outside your control, and it can obliterate your business if you don't detect it in time and create your own space in the new environment that is taking shape. A contemporary case in point is the decline of Dell Computer, one of the world's most celebrated success stories. For three decades Michael Dell and his leadership team prospered with their "made-to-order model" as the heart of the business. It enabled them to know precisely which components were needed when, so they could meet customer demand quickly and with minimal extra components in inventory. With its high velocity of inventory turns, low margins, and low prices, Dell gained market share; with negative working capital,[2] it was a net cash generator on the order of a billion dollars every quarter. Dell became the highly profitable industry leader in market share.

Then Dell got hit with a double whammy. One was operational: IBM's sale of its PC business to Lenovo in 2004. When the first two CEOs of Lenovo, both from the United States, didn't work out, people said the Chinese company would never succeed. Then Yang Yuanging, a Chinese businessman and longtime leader at Lenovo, became CEO in 2009. He took an unusual approach by focusing on lower cost and innovation at the same time, and Lenovo attained number one market share in the world against Dell and HP. Lenovo's lower prices put a squeeze on Dell's margins and cash flow, resulting in a significant decline in Dell's stock price.

Dell might have overcome this operational challenge, but at roughly the same time a killer structural change occurred: the introduction of tablets (Android based and Apple's iPad) and smart phones. Like everyone else in the personal computer industry, Dell was blindsided by this development. It was one of the most dramatic shifts ever in that industry and signaled a fundamental decline in the desktop and laptop market. Dell's great run came to an end because structural change meant that its core competencies were no longer a competitive advantage. (On a personal note, I have known Michael Dell for a long time, and no one should write him and his company off. He has taken Dell Computer private to give himself the freedom to place big bets on the future.)

Few industries are exempt from the threat of structural uncertainty—even basic and fragmented ones such as the taxicab business. Its economics have essentially not changed in decades of operating with regulated fares and high-priced medallions, which limit the number of competitors. For drivers and fleet owners, the major problems have been operating issues such as fuel costs and arguing with regulators about how to split the revenues. Now the model is being challenged by increasingly popular real-time ride-sharing companies such as Uber and Lyft, in which customers using mobile device apps arrange trips with operators of privately owned cars. They began to appear around 2012 in tech-savvy San Francisco; by mid-2014 they had spread to major cities throughout the United States and around the globe. Regulators initially tried to ban the outfits, but more and more of them have yielded to the new reality of a service in wide demand. The California Public Utilities Commission, has even come up with a label that may become the standard definition: "transportation network companies." European governments have been friendlier to the established operators, but as popular demand grows, fleet owners and drivers alike will be looking at a structural phenomenon that could decimate their business.

A structural uncertainty does not arise as suddenly as it seems; more often than not there are early warning signals that go unnoticed. Nokia had a fantastic brand, was highly profitable, and built dominant market share. Its near-demise—with an almost vertical, steep decline in revenues, margins, cash, and market share—took less than three years. The bend in the road was caused by Apple, which offered a new, compelling consumer experience. It was so enormously different that the consumer not only paid a high price but waited in line to gain access to it.

Nokia was taken by surprise—but it shouldn't have been. My personal interaction with its CEO two years before the introduction of the iPhone indicated that the company was aware of it, with a particular early warning signal coming from people at Nokia reading Apple's patent filings. But the leadership team found it hard to believe that a computer company would go into the cell phone business and thought that Apple would not be a threat even if it did, because it wasn't big enough to pose a serious challenge. True, Apple had successfully entered consumer electronics with the iPod, but that was a high-priced product with a fat margin. Apple's phone would presumably be similarly positioned and not likely to gain a substantial market share. Apple would also have trouble going through telecommunication carriers, which Nokia dominated. Since Nokia was the largest carrier, had the largest market share, and had the best-recognized brand, the leadership team reasoned that they would be able to catch up even if they did miss a beat. What confounded Nokia was the uniqueness of the iPhone and the ferocity with which Apple scaled up, creating a new customer experience and a new high-price, high-margin mass market that superseded the old one. The new market rapidly expanded, and its rate of growth increased.

Elon Musk has created an unexpected and possibly significant uncertainty for the auto industry. Until recently the money the automakers spent developing electric cars basically sustained a mixture of speculation and public relations. But the recent critical and popular success of Musk's Tesla has gotten their attention. Initially it was considered an outlier, a toy for affluent greenies. But it soon became evident that Musk's breakthrough in the design and manufacturing of batteries had greater potential. He was able to widen the market and begin scaling up; in 2014 the company was expected to deliver some thirty-five thousand near-luxury cars. Daimler and Toyota have bought Tesla powertrain systems and invested in the company. Will this create a bend in the road for brands in luxury and near-luxury segments—Cadillac, Lincoln, Jaguar, Mercedes Benz, and the upper price models of Volkswagen—in which BMW has taken the lead and is on the attack? Or could it create an even bigger market? In June 2014 Tesla announced that it would make its patents widely available to automakers in the interest of speeding up electric car development around the world. China under President Xi seems to be taking its pollution problems seriously. That market alone could create an electrifying bend in the road for the global auto industry. Automakers everywhere now have a whole new potential business to consider and factor into their plans as either a boon or a threat.

The opportunity in structural uncertainty was summed up for me by G. M. Rao, the chairman of GMR, India's largest infrastructure business. He once told me that every bend in the road contains a message about a future growth trajectory that someone could explore and exploit if he or she looked at it through a different lens without being controlled by an existing core competency. Since the opportunity is by definition totally new, the instinctive reaction more often than not is "we know nothing about it; it doesn't fit with our core concept of the business and our core capabilities." The leaders who succeed *because* of uncertainty realize that a world in flux creates new possibilities and lowers the entry barriers. They are the attackers. They see clearly, move decisively, and act.

CHAPTER 3

The Mathematical Corporation: The Algorithmic Revolution and the Rise of the Math House

THE SINGLE GREATEST instrument of change—the one that is creating major uncertainties and opportunities for an ever-growing universe of today's businesses—is the advancement of the mathematical tools called algorithms and their related sophisticated software. Never before has so much mental power been computerized and made available to so many—power to deconstruct and predict patterns and changes in everything from consumer behavior and human health to the maintenance requirements and operating lifetimes of industrial machinery. In combination with other technological factors, algorithms are dramatically changing both the structure of the global economy and the lifestyles of individual people. (The others include digitization, the Internet, broadband mobility, sensors, and faster and cheaper-by-the-day data-crunching abilities.)

Algorithms and the decision engines they drive process enormous amounts of data, far beyond what the brain can handle, at light speed. They run through iterations that can number in the millions, examining options and second- and third-order consequences of a particular decision option, then producing outputs for a human mind to accept, reject, or have redone. Just as human beings can learn from experience and improve or change, algorithms can be programmed to learn from the outcomes of their decisions and improve subsequent decisions or predictions.

All these advances have been made in the last few decades, yet the use of algorithms is already fracturing time-tested business models and creating trailblazing new ones. Algorithms are most prominent so far for their role in radically transforming retailing, creating new and highly interactive relationships between businesses and their customers by literally making it possible for giant corporations to deal with customers as individuals. Now the revolution is entering a new and vastly expansive stage in which machines communicate with other machines without human intervention, learning through artificial intelligence and making consistent decisions based on prescribed rules and processed through algorithms. This capability has rapidly expanded into potential connections between billions and billions of devices in the ever-expanding Internet of Things (IoT), which integrates machines and devices with networked sensors and software. That's what allows consumers to use their smart phones to program the thermostat settings and check on their pets at home from just about anywhere. More sophisticated ones remotely monitor and adjust industrial machinery and manage supply chains. Machine-to-machine communication and learning also helps people increase their capability and capacity and the speed of their decisions. We have barely scratched the surface of the potential uses, and the growth opportunities of this bend in the road can be immense for those who seize the opportunity.

Companies that have the new mathematical capabilities possess a huge advantage over those that don't, even those that have been highly successful in the past. They are not just digitized—they are *math houses*, as I call them, and they are creating structural uncertainty for all industries and the companies within them. Google, Facebook, and Amazon were created as mathematical corporations; they were, as some say, born digital. Apple became a math corporation after Steve Jobs returned as CEO. This trend will accelerate. Legacy companies that can't make the shift will be vulnerable to digital competitors. Business leaders need competence in digitization—at least enough to know the right questions to ask the experts, along with the imagination to find ways for mathematics to help them redesign the consumer experience.

Indeed, one of the biggest changes the algorithmic approach brings to both businesses and consumers is a rich new level of interactivity. The customer experience for many legacy companies is often secondhand and more often than not thirdhand. A company's offerings are, for example, bought by distributor X, who in turn sells to retailer Y, who sells to an individual. In today's online math houses, by contrast, actual users are more and more often interacting with the company—buying directly and providing feedback without any intermediaries. The companies can track and even predict consumer preferences in real time and adjust strategies and offerings on the run to meet their changing demands, which gives consumers leverage they never had before.

Decisions made through the use of algorithms enable a filter-free, back-and-forth dialogue between the producer and the individual consumer, delivering information or decisions in real time consistently and reliably, according to predetermined decision rules embedded in the algorithm. For those decisions that do require human judgment, the machines kick the issue to a person. The data accumulated from these interactions can be used for all manner of purposes. For example, the end-to-end consumer experience has a large number of touch points, each of which—whether human, digital, or Web related—can be predictable or unpredictable. A company can map out all these touch points in extreme detail and gather information at each one. A math engine can then generate insights to guide managerial decisions about such things as innovation, new product development, and resource allocation. Such analyses of user touch points can be done continuously in real time or through mathematical sampling over time, not just for one event.

The data can also be used as a diagnostic tool—for example, they can reveal signals and seeds of potential external change and help identify uncertainties and new opportunities. They can point to anomalies from past trends and whether they are becoming a pattern and help spot new needs or trends that are emerging and could make your business obsolete.

Indeed, the math house is shaping up as a new stage in the evolution of relations between businesses and consumers. The first stage, before the Industrial Revolution, was one-to-one transactions between artisans and their customers. Then came the era of mass production and mass markets, followed by the segmenting of markets and semicustomization of the buying experience. With companies such as Amazon able to collect and manage information on the entire experience of a customer, the math house now can focus on each customer as an individual. In a manner of speaking, we are evolving back to the artisan model, in which a market segment comprises one individual.

The ability to connect the corporation to the customer experience and touch points in real time has deep implications for the organization of the future. It speeds decision making and allows leaders to flatten the organization, in some cases cutting layers by half. A large proportion of traditional middle management jobs—managers managing managers—will disappear, while the content of those jobs that remain will radically alter. The company's overhead will be reduced by an order of magnitude; while creative experts are high priced, there will be an enormous reduction in the cost of management as well as that of low-skilled labor. In addition, performance metrics will be totally redesigned and transparent, enhancing collaboration in a corporation or its ecosystems across silos, geographies, time zones, and cultures.

Redefining an Industrial Icon

GE, one of only five firms on the original Dow Jones index still in existence, is now essentially turning itself into a math house. It had been a leader among industrial companies in generating new business by servicing the equipment it sold, from jet engines and locomotives to turbines and medical imaging equipment. Now it has parlayed that legacy into a huge and transformational leap into what it calls the Industrial Internet, a term it coined. As of mid-2014, this quintessential industrial company got about two-thirds of its $250 billion backlog in orders from services based on its mathematical intellectual property.

The big shift for GE management began around 2010, when they saw more clearly that IBM had been moving into the industrial space GE and other players occupied. IBM provided sophisticated software that worked in conjunction with industrial equipment and influenced customers' purchases of that equipment. Leaders at GE saw an opportunity for new revenue in the software space, first to influence purchase decisions, and second to influence the design of its equipment and services. Software promised very high margins and low investment compared with the equipment itself. GE began to expand into the Industrial Internet. It moved decisively. Starting in 2011 it assembled a staff in Silicon Valley of experts in sophisticated software and algorithms. The cost was small for a company of GE's size but vast in its ramifications: since then GE has become the leader in the Industrial Internet. Along with ATT, Cisco, IBM, and Intel, it was a founder of the Industrial Internet Consortium, organized in 2014 to hasten development of the IoT, and through continuing collaborations it is expanding and shaping the space.

GE's plunge into the Industrial Internet has opened up new trajectories of profitable growth from its expertise in areas such as medical equipment, turbines, oil and gas, electrical grids, locomotives, and aircraft engines. Customers benefit from reduced downtime of their highly capital-intensive fixed assets. GE has increased its hold on the services business, which has high margins and low capital intensity and high customer retention. It not only uses the Industrial Internet to improve the profitability of its own products and services, but also creates new demand by sharing its sophisticated software packages and algorithms with competitors. Greater interconnectivity expands usage, opening up an exponential growth trajectory for GE and enlarging its piece of an expanding pie. The company is already reaping the benefits of increased market share, faster revenue growth, and higher margins. In one segment of power equipment, for example, it has improved margins and is now ahead of its strongest competitor, with a huge jump in market share from 30 to 48 percent.

GE's newly built expertise in software and algorithms has recast the entire company for the twenty-first century, positioning it—in CEO Jeffrey Immelt's words—"to drive results through uncertainty." He has sharpened the company's focus by unloading GE Capital, keeping only the parts that will serve the company as a specialty finance division, and the legacy appliance business. This recasting is triggering changes in the selection and promotion of people, the content of training, career development plans, and operating mechanisms such as reviews in GE's legendary operating system. At the same time, it is reducing costs across the company. His actions provide a textbook example of finding opportunity in uncertainty.

To take advantage of uncertainty, you must make the use of algorithms part of your vocabulary tomorrow as much as, say, profit margins and the supply chain are today. And your executive team must understand their role in growing the business. This is a factor so powerful that I feel confident in stating that any organization that is not a math house now or is unable to become one soon is already a legacy company. The transformation has nothing to do with how young or old the company is, but rather with how effectively it deals on a timely basis with the new paradigm. It will require more than hiring new kinds of expertise and grafting new skills onto the existing organization. Many companies will need to substantially change the way they are organized, managed, and led.

CHAPTER 4

Searching for Early Warning Signals

MANY BUSINESS LEADERS live with the constant but unspoken fear that the "givens" of their industry could suddenly change, and they won't see the change coming. I observe this behavior almost daily through the actions—and especially the inaction—of people up and down the hierarchy in every industry. There's a long list of prominent leaders who ignored or failed to see warning signals of structural change, from the apocryphal buggy-whip makers who didn't believe the automobile could threaten them to the Nokia executives who looked at the patent filings for the iPhone but discounted its possible significance for their business. Often the signals emanate not from within your immediate ecosystem, but from some outlier or oddity. When Napster appeared with its sophisticated software and algorithms that allowed people to share music files online, the music industry assumed it would only be a matter of time until the courts put an end to what was essentially piracy. Then Steve Jobs struck a deal to buy songs and distribute them through iTunes to Apple's breakthrough product, the iPod. Industry titans didn't pick up the early warning signal Napster sent, nor did they reset their path fast enough. Power shifted within the value chain as high-margin CD sales fell drastically, dragging total industry revenues down with them.

People often miss these early warning signals because they're "flying at low altitude," immersed in the daily operating details of the business. Amid the financial crisis in 2009, I was meeting in Turkey with "Michael Barry," the owner of an equipment manufacturing company with $1 billion in revenue, who had been energetically roaming the world and acquiring new customers. Now he was visiting his local leaders in Turkey for a quarterly review. He arrived to bad news: the team was at risk of missing their quarterly sales targets because customers were running into serious trouble getting financing. Usually they would work with one bank to get the loans they needed to buy his company's capital equipment. But because the government had been forcing banks to strengthen their balance sheets, customers had to work with four, five, even six banks and sometimes still did not get what they needed. A big sale had just fallen through at the eleventh hour because one of six banks had pulled out, and then another. Local management wanted to know if the parent company could extend more financing to seal the deal.

This wasn't the first sign of trouble. Michael had faced a similar problem in Brazil and the United States the previous month, when his company was forced to finance sales from its balance sheet. In fact, bankers were cutting back everywhere—but he was still holding production steady, and cash was being depleted. Within another month the business was unable to keep up the financing, and inventory began to pile up. Michael had missed the signals because he wasn't searching at a high enough altitude to recognize the global financial forces and connect the dots. Ultimately the balance sheet became so strained that he had no choice but to scale down production, lay off employees, and shrink the business substantially.

By contrast, let me tell you about "Bill Smith," who leads a global line of business based in the United States as part of "Vitalmetrics," a medical devices company. He is responsible for worldwide profits, market share, and sales for his business unit. Recently the news had broken that the Chinese government was accusing GlaxoSmithKline (GSK), one of the world's leading pharmaceutical companies, of bribery and inflated prices. Bill was always scanning for developments that might turn out to have a big impact on his unit, even if they didn't seem to be important or directly related to his business, and he made a habit of testing out his perceptions with others. He and I were meeting over dinner on a July evening in 2013 after a session I had taught on global trends, and Bill was full of questions.

He explained that he had picked up the news about GSK and was trying to put it into the context of broader changes he had observed in China, particularly since President Xi had announced that he would make fighting corruption one of his most important initiatives. China had long-standing anticorruption laws on its books, but they had not been enforced because of the country's ineffective legal system.

Bill's hypothesis was that the government might be making an example of GSK and perhaps other non-Chinese companies to show that regulators were now prepared to take action. "Do you think this action is a shot across the bow?" Bill asked me. "How many companies might be targeted? And would we be included? I've already contacted our corporate chief risk officer and general counsel. We've been very vigilant, but even an investigation will give us a black eye with the board of directors and the media."

I complimented Bill for picking up what might be an early warning signal from outside his industry in the geopolitical sphere, and pushed him to go further. "What are the implications of this for your total global P&L? Does it have any impact?" Bill thought about that for a moment. His unit was Vitalmetrics's second largest producer of profit, and its fastest-growing unit. Revenues in the United States and Europe were basically flat. The best prospect for growth of his unit was China. Bill had projected 30 percent growth in revenue and 20 percent growth in profit per year in China over the next three years. In fact, Bill and his bosses were counting on it. He had had a stellar career for the past twenty years, and while his future looked bright at the moment, he knew it would be tough to survive a major shortfall.

"If the government does find evidence of corruption that caused inflated prices, I suppose it will force prices down across the industry. And would our industry be next?"

"What would you do if that happens?" I asked.

There was a long pause. "Rough out a plan for offsetting the losses," Bill said. "I'll have to get the team to scout for new sources of revenue and profits, reset the targets, and reallocate some resources to other parts of the world." Another pause, and then—forcefully: "I need to get our creativity into high gear."

We spent the rest of the dinner talking about conditions in China, imagining different directions things could go and their potential consequences. Bill left the restaurant upbeat and ready for the challenge. He had raised his altitude and picked up a signal about a possible change to his industry and had already begun to think about how to deal with it. He would watch how geopolitical events unfold with a keen sense of purpose and keep scanning the external environment for signals of accelerating change or a change of direction. Importantly, he saw the uncertainty he faced in China not just as a source of anxiety, but as a possible opportunity.

———

THE ATTACKER'S ADVANTAGE is the ability to detect ahead of others those forces that are radically reshaping your marketplace, then position your business to make the next move first. The rest of this book gives you the tools and examples you need to go on the attack, to pinpoint the sources of uncertainty, remove some of their mystery, define a path forward, and make the necessary frequent adjustments to steer your organization along it. Uncertainty is not something to fear, but rather something to immerse yourself in, because in it lie the possibilities you can combine to create something new and immensely valuable. The more you embrace uncertainty and practice the skills to deal with it, the more self-confidence you will develop and the better prepared you will be to lead.

CHECKLIST FOR PART I

✓ How aware are you that structural change is occurring more frequently? Does it worry you, or do you see opportunity in it? Do you consider it part of your job as a leader to detect it? Do you consider it part of your job to create it?

✓ Do you pause to consider whether operating problems are signs of structural change?

✓ Do you scan the external landscape the way Bill Smith did (see chapter 4)? Is your altitude high enough to see above your industry to geopolitical and other macro factors? Do you have a disciplined routine for rising above the daily details and sharpening your mental antennae to identify bends in the road sooner? Is your team doing so as well?

✓ Are you tracking companies that are using mathematics and advanced computing power to transform their business, even if they are outside your industry? Are you imagining how some of them might destroy your industry and reshape your market space?

✓ Are you prepared to accept the reality that uncertainty is here to stay? Do you realize that you may need to make bold decisions even when some of the factors you base them on are still not clear?

✓ Are you psychologically and organizationally prepared to convert uncertainty into breakthrough opportunities? This is the new leadership imperative.

PART II

BUILDING PERCEPTUAL ACUITY

CHAPTER 5

Identifying the Catalysts
of Structural Change

HOW MANY TIMES have you heard someone say something like "Ted Turner could see it, but others couldn't," referring to his creation of a national cable television network and CNN, the first-ever twenty-four-hour news station? Or ask "How could they have missed it?" after SONY's leaders slept through the dawn of digital music: a stunning lack of perceptual acuity from the company whose Walkman was one of the groundbreaking products of the 1980s.

Perceptual acuity is your human radar for seeing through the fog of uncertainty so you can act before others do. Turner had it; Sony's leaders didn't. Few upcoming leaders have exercised it, because it is not yet a common part of daily leadership practice or development. They are looking from the inside out, through a narrow aperture for things that fit with what they know. Only a very small percentage look at their businesses from the outside in and peer over the horizon to pick up signals that could be harbingers of change.

One of the earliest warnings is the emergence of a catalyst. This is a person with exceptional perceptual acuity who seizes upon a force or combination of forces—for example, linking a demographic trend with an existing technology. Typically he or she is a creative thinker, unconstrained by conventional wisdom. Such a person mulls over his perceptions, compares them with the views of others in his social networks, tosses hypotheses around in his mind—a good deal of the time unconsciously—and gets excited about the possibility of new opportunities. And importantly, he acts on what he hypothesizes. Catalysts are doers who take risks based partly on fact and partly on their imagination about what could happen when forces combine in what others might later call a convergence. The catalyst, in fact, is the one who often creates the convergence.

Once again: sharp perceptual acuity is a requisite leadership ability, and noticing or sensing events, trends, and anomalies over the horizon—anything that is new compared with what you have known, no matter how weak the signal—is a skill of leadership practice.

Turner's ability to spot what was new and different was evident early in his career. His first insight was to imagine the advantages of combining satellite transmission and the then nascent cable network, even when the pieces were not yet fully in place. He had ventured into TV by buying a small UHF station in Atlanta in 1970, soon after taking over his father's billboard advertising business. The plan he devised was to transform his tiny local station into a national one by beaming its signals to a satellite, then downloading them to dishes across the country and transmitting the captured signals to viewers via cable. Before he could create this national grid, he faced a hurdle: the Federal Communications Commission (FCC), which granted separate licenses to each locality. Not to be dissuaded, Turner pressed the US Congress to intervene, arguing persuasively that his plan would give consumers more choice. The FCC approved his proposal for a national license, and his local station grew into a superstation practically overnight. Turner found clever ways to fill the hours with programming, such as the now common practice of running old movies and TV shows, and he went so far as to buy the Atlanta Braves to ensure that his TV station would be allowed to cover the games.

In the 1970s he zeroed in on a flaw in the major TV networks' news coverage. Why, he asked, should consumers have to get it at a set hour, typically 6:00 p.m.? Why not make it available at any time, day or night? CNN, with its pioneering twenty-four-hour news format, became a major player in the broadcasting industry.

Turner was known to shoot from the hip, but his boldest moves were rooted in his perceptual acuity. Robert Wright, the former president of NBC, said of Turner, "He sees the obvious before most people do. We all look at the same picture, but Ted sees what you don't see. And after he sees it, it becomes obvious to everyone."[3] Importantly, he acted on his perceptions and thus became a catalyst of change.

The events or new technologies a catalyst picks up on are what I call *seeds*. The seeds might lie fallow for a long time until a catalyst picks them up and does something with them—cultivates them, if you will—and they blossom. For example, a patent can be a seed, yet holding a large number of patents makes no impact. It takes a catalyst to see how that patent can be used in an innovative way that hits a sweet spot in the market. Then the tectonic plates shift: structural change of material importance to your business occurs and redefines money making, blows apart business models, and reorders many of the players in the industry or obliterates it.

Though perceptual acuity is a native talent for the Turners of this world, you can cultivate it by watching such people and adopting the routine and disciplined practice of looking over the horizon and searching for new ideas, events, technologies, or trends—things that an imaginative person could combine to meet an unmet need or create a totally new one. This will also sharpen your capacity to see trends developing before others do. Hone your perceptual acuity, and you will be able to identify the catalyst and visualize future outcomes if she gains traction. Could this person find a way to overcome what everyone else thinks is an impossible hurdle? It is those kinds of creative breakthroughs that can alter or destroy one or more industries or create a new one. Someone watching Turner's moves early on might have concluded that the licensing process would drag on for years. But it would have been wise to consider that the FCC's policy could change. Your perceptual acuity would then have you watching for signals of further change, and if you thought the catalyst was succeeding, you could ask yourself: Could I ride on this wave, be on the offensive, and shape it to my company's advantage?

A personal experience in my early years showed me that a catalyst can be more important in turning a discovery into a commercial success than the person who actually makes the discovery. A wealthy and highly respected physician lived in my hometown in India, and although my family was substantially lower in income and therefore had no social interaction with his family, he paid my father a visit just before I left home to go to university. The doctor had heard that I would be the first person from our town to go to the engineering school at Banaras University, the MIT of India. His two daughters would be attending the women's college on the same campus, and he wanted me to meet them. A year later he introduced me to Bishnu Atal, who, in an arranged marriage, was the husband-to-be of one of the daughters, and to my surprise I was invited to the wedding.

The couple moved to New Jersey in the early 1960s, where Atal worked as a scientist for Bell Labs. When I went to America two years later, the doctor suggested that I visit his daughter and son-in-law. That's how I learned about Atal's research into speech recognition technology. He had been working day and night and succeeded in making a breakthrough in developing this powerful tool, garnering many awards and worldwide recognition. But despite its fame among the technical cognoscenti, Atal's invention languished in commercial obscurity for about a decade. Only then did a business leader and engineer at Texas Instruments, Paul Breedlove, pick it up and, with an initial budget of $25,000 and Dr. Atal as a consultant, create a device for children called "Speak and Spell," a learning toy that became a huge success. Breedlove had the perceptual acuity to notice the potential of a technology no one else had paid attention to; he is the catalyst who converted it into a commercial product that paved the way for many more applications. Since then, of course, speech recognition has become ubiquitous, and others have developed it further and combined it with other technological advances, even to the extent that a company can identify a customer's emotional state by his or her voice and customize its services accordingly.

The greatest test of perceptual acuity is the ability to pick out catalysts and seeds even when the signals are weak, meaning that they are intermittent or seem irrelevant. Retailers lacking perceptual acuity might, for example, have underestimated the significance of Apple's bringing in Angela Ahrendts as senior vice president of retail and online stores in early 2014. What sort of nuttiness, one might ask, was it to hire the highly successful CEO of Burberry, one of the world's best brands, to run a mere division—one that is not even Apple's largest revenue generator? The perceptively acute person would immediately ask questions: Why would such a creative and accomplished executive give up a role as CEO to take on a lesser job? Is she perhaps a catalyst who will totally reconceptualize what the stores do? What might her intentions be? One hypothesis would be that she may convert them into a mecca for fashion and luxury, not just for hardware and software. People in the fashion business, Ahrendts's former industry, should sharpen their antennae to observe her moves and detect what might lie ahead. They should be particularly vigilant about the kind of people she is hiring—designers, retailers, technologists?— since those decisions will signal a future trajectory. They should also be aware that she is highly proficient in the new math of commerce—fully conversant with algorithms, she took the initiative to work with global software giant SAP to design software that creates a virtual dressing room, allowing a customer to view herself in a garment on her mobile device. They should add to their mental databases the fact that Apple invited fashion journalists to its September 2014 unveiling of the Apple Watch.

Many catalysts develop over time but show their true colors early on, and they often repeat their performance, so it's worth the effort to search for those who are emerging or have a track record: often the critic or the gadfly, the graduate student who stirs controversy among the "experts," the researcher who comes up with a technical breakthrough, or the young entrepreneur who rockets to success. Once you have identified a potential catalyst, you can try to interact with her or track her activity and form hypotheses about what she will do next, what pieces she is trying to assemble, and what missing piece she might be seeking, bearing in mind that catalysts have an unshakeable belief in their vision. Such scraps of information become early warning signals. By identifying the catalyst driving a major shift, you can form an idea of how big it might be and its timing.

Here are five examples of catalysts, discussed in the following sections:

- The man who reshaped the auto market—twice
- Pioneers of the Internet
- Digital-era venture capitalist: Andreessen's act two
- The industrial archaeologist
- Crusaders

The Man Who Reshaped the Auto Market—Twice

A catalyst has to be in the right environment before he can ignite something. Hal Sperlich, a product planner at Ford in the 1960s, was the chief architect of the Mustang, which he developed with the support of Lee Iaccoca, Ford Division general manager at the time. The Mustang created a major new segment, with an "automotive home run that sold a record 418,000 vehicles in its first year, striking a chord in the American market because it combined something that consumers were not expecting: a compact car that was exciting and affordable."[4]

Sperlich was obsessed with finding the anomalies of social change in demographics. He did a meticulous analysis of emerging lifestyles in America, and soon after launch of the Mustang concluded that families needed something between a car and a truck: a relatively compact but spacious vehicle in which families could transport kids and all their stuff. But despite his success with the Mustang, Ford's senior management blew him off harshly. Henry Ford II, then the chairman and CEO, had no interest in a radical, unproven concept, especially one that would have a front-wheel drive platform; Ford had none and didn't want to invest in developing one; he told Iacocca to fire Sperlich. Chrysler, which was in a downward spiral in cash flow and market share, hired Sperlich. Not long after, Iacocca was also fired. He followed his close friend to Chrysler and became the CEO. Iacocca adopted the idea of the minivan. It was a success from day one, ensured Chrysler's survival, and went on to create an enormous new automotive segment as other automakers followed suit.

Pioneers of the Internet

The Internet was born in government and academia, but its wider use was ushered in by a series of catalysts. The first was Tim Berners-Lee, who while at CERN, the European Particle Physics Institute, developed the World Wide Web. Then Mark Andreessen, while still a student at the University of Illinois, opened up the Web for general public use by creating a popular browser that made the vast range of information on the Internet easier for ordinary people to navigate. He cofounded the company Netscape to commercialize it. We all know what has happened since then: a growing tranche of the human race finds it impossible to imagine life without the Internet.

Microsoft's Bill Gates was one who didn't see that Andreessen was a catalyst. When Gates did get around to recognizing Netscape's threat to his personal computer software business, he quickly created his own browser, Internet Explorer. Gates didn't just sell a competing browser; he ate up Netscape's market share by including Explorer in Windows software at no cost. Subsequent antitrust suits and fines in the United States and Europe couldn't stop Explorer's advance.

Digital-Era Venture Capitalist:
Andreessen's Act Two

Given the ubiquity of the Internet, the accessibility of mathematics, and the infrastructure of the Cloud—which is cost-free to users—we now have lots of young people in universities from Silicon Valley and Bangalore to Singapore and Israel with tremendous information and connectivity at their disposal. Surely these emerging clusters of technology throughout the world will produce new catalysts who will make new breakthroughs. Many Silicon Valley companies are identifying such catalysts as a regular practice. Mark Andreessen, through his firm Andreessen Horowitz, is actively courted by some of the largest legacy Fortune 50 companies. He is a digital-era venture-capitalist catalyst who differs from the legacy venture capitalists of the personal computer era in that he is tuned in to the use of algorithms and sophisticated software, primarily using the Cloud. Ideas come to him from "kids" who are young digital natives seeking to launch their ideas. In the center of new ideas, he can see what's truly novel and a potential breakthrough and match the upstarts to large partners or buyers. You could call Andreessen a serial catalyst. He and his firm connect the young upstarts with new ideas to his network of big-company CEOs—people like Larry Page of Google, Mark Zuckerberg of Facebook, and Meg Whitman of HP—all of whom have the wherewithal to fund promising road-benders and scale them up rapidly.

The Industrial Archaeologist

A catalyst can even revive a "dead" technology—one that seems to have no capacity to produce something that is novel and compelling—by finding a use for it in a new need, market, or consumer experience. That's what Steve Jobs did with "Gorilla Glass," a three-decades-old glass-making technology developed by Corning that had essentially been mothballed.

I saw how tracking Jobs's interests could provide a heads-up on the next industry-shattering innovation at a dinner I was attending after the iPhone was introduced. Among the guests were several CEOs, including Wendell Weeks, the CEO and chairman of Corning Glass. People were of course fascinated with the phenomenon of the iPhone, and Weeks told us that one day Jobs called and asked if he could meet him at the Corning Glass headquarters in upstate New York. Ever on the lookout for ways to make products better, Jobs had been looking for a tougher and thinner glass for the iPhone's screen. He had learned that several decades earlier Corning actually produced an ultra-strong annealed glass called Gorilla Glass with the characteristics he desired, but that the plant producing it had been shut down years before. Jobs persuaded Weeks to reopen it and got his glass—along with a relationship that promised to put him at the head of the line for any new kinds of glass Corning's extraordinary research capabilities would create in the future.

The impressive and rapid scaling up of the use of Gorilla Glass was a clear early warning signal that it could change many other strategies and business models. It was an observable fact that this glass would have widespread uses in other industries, and that with further development and highly sophisticated software, it could create other whiz-bang communication products. Why not a transparent refrigerator that could transmit messages written on it directly to a provider of merchandise, who could replenish supplies? Or a giant screen that can detect hand motions, not just touch, and can be written on, allowing people around the globe to collaborate virtually? I have actually seen such screens in use at the Microsoft Envision Center. People can see each other, exchange data and pictures, and design a product simultaneously across boundaries using the intelligent devices of which this glass is an important part.

Crusaders

A catalyst can be a gadfly such as Ralph Nader, an energetic critic of American business and politics for fifty years. He changed not only the worldwide auto industry but many others as well. Nader's book *Unsafe at Any Speed* was a pioneering analysis of the automakers' failure to think about the safety of their products. The storm that followed was instrumental in bringing General Motors (then the world's biggest automobile producer) to its knees and changing the expectations of consumers and government regulators about product safety. Every automaker in the world must now provide safety features, and as a consequence, his critique created multi-billion-dollar opportunities in a totally new market segment that evolved and rapidly grew under the rubric of safety systems.

TRW, for example, developed a substantial source of revenue, growth, and profit from becoming the number-one supplier of airbags and other safety systems to Ford and a major supplier to General Motors. Ruben Mettler, a longtime CEO of TRW and well-respected engineer, saw the opportunity. TRW's defense division was widely recognized for its technological innovation, and Mettler realized that some of its technology could be applied to passenger restraint systems. The company made the necessary investment and became the world leader. Volvo, a niche importer whose customers prized its sturdily built cars, repositioned itself as a unique brand, differentiated by its attention to safety, and secured a much larger place in the market. Safety concerns created a huge opportunity for DuPont, which developed a methodology for safety-focused cultural change and now has a major division that helps companies worldwide improve their practices.

As safety rose on the agenda of public concerns, other catalysts broadened its applications to include many more industries and the plants they run. Today safety instructions appear on an ever-growing galaxy of products and in just about any place where people gather. Safety has become a top criterion for developers in selecting construction companies. When I was serving on the board of Dallas-based Austin Industries, a leading regional builder of buildings and airports, we discussed safety as a regular practice; Austin's safety record became a competitive advantage in bidding.

Unsafe at Any Speed is close to being a picture-perfect example of the two sides of structural uncertainty. The big car companies saw it as a threat; other players recognized an opportunity and went on the attack. And the book's larger message became woven into society as a whole.

And who knows who the next Nader will be? Perhaps Michael Bloomberg, the billionaire who became the famously health-conscious mayor of New York City. There, among other things, he tried to outlaw large cups of sugary soft drinks (though the courts struck his law down) and made restaurant chains post calorie counts on their menus, a demand that other cities are emulating and that became part of the Affordable Care Act of 2010. But let's not be US centric. Catalysts were at work in Mexico when the government imposed a stiff tax on sugary carbonated beverages in that country.

Shouldn't you ask yourself whether these catalysts could change the outlook for your business—or provide it with a new opportunity?

———

PRACTICE YOUR PERCEPTUAL acuity by watching for catalysts in or outside your industry, regardless of your job or organizational level. Your judgment will improve by checking it after the fact and reflecting on where you were or were not correct, and why. As your acuity sharpens, you'll spot catalysts sooner and begin to see the world as they see it: full of new possibilities and opportunities. The next chapter will help you see what's new and different even sooner.

CHAPTER 6

Seeing What Catalysts See

AS YOU DEVELOP your perceptual acuity, you will become more attuned to interesting new ideas, events, technology developments, and trends. You'll expand your capacity to see the landscape from multiple angles, discern what's important, and speculate about how you could shape it by engaging other people in this task. You'll not only benefit from the diverse points of view, but also build your team's ability to detect change sooner and create the next bend in the road.

Train yourself to stand back from your business and its environment. In particular, look for the larger significance of anomalies, contradictions, and oddities: things that depart from or challenge familiar patterns and differ from what you have known or believed. For example, if you are in the medical devices business—which includes companies such as GE, Siemens, Phillips, and the SonoSite division of

FujiFilm—you are surely aware that the expanding use of mobile phones and devices such as smart watches could be your next bend in the road, because it provides other ways to measure what is happening to a patient besides X-rays, CT scans, and MRIs. Regular transmission of the information to health-care providers can track changes in a person's health, especially if there is a perception of deterioration. Now Apple and Google are recruiting physicians and other health-care professionals, especially those with domain knowledge in the diagnosis of disease. Will they be catalysts who might initiate change in some segments of the health-care industry?

When Anne Wojcicki cofounded 23andMe in 2007, the basic idea behind the biotech company was to give consumers information about their own genetic makeup for a relatively low cost. At the same time, 23andMe would collect genetic information from customers who agreed to share it and make the database available to pharmaceutical companies and other medical researchers to improve health care for everyone. It was a hot idea from this former Google employee, until the Food and Drug Administration (FDA) banned the company from going directly to the public. The agency was not convinced the tests were accurate and worried that consumers lacking the expertise to interpret the results might pursue expensive, unneeded testing and potentially harmful or unnecessary treatments. Is this the end for 23andMe and other genetic testing services like it? The answer depends in part on how much and how soon consumers want to take control of their health and medical information, and whether scientific advances make the tests more reliable. The Affordable Care Act is already accelerating a shift to consumer power, and 23andMe is continuing to work with the FDA. The odds are that Wojcicki or another catalyst will find a way to overcome the barrier; history shows that if a technology works and the market demands it, constraints will eventually be demolished.

Some people see the impact of a catalyst too narrowly and not in terms of its broader, more durable influence. I was in a board meeting at Seagrams, which at the time owned Universal Music, the world's largest music company, when Napster had just recently come onto the scene. When the topic came up, some people in the room were clearly on edge, fearful that Napster's success would be an enormous blow to Universal. Some directors had the clear intention to shut it down through legal means with no expense spared, and the legal experts presented several ways to go after it aggressively. As the discussion was coming to a close, one director paused and glanced around the room. In a hushed voice he said, "No law can prevent a social change."

What to Watch For

You no doubt get information from many sources—from print and video media to interactions through Facebook, Twitter, and Linked-in. Your reading or listening provokes new ideas in you or a recombination of information you have already stored. Out of this hubbub you need to be on the alert for what is new and what is an anomaly, contradiction, or oddity. Often you are able to crystallize what you've learned in fewer than thirty seconds, and it takes equally little time to toss it around in your mind and be intellectually honest about whether it matters. Is this a seed someone will do something with? If it picks up steam, will it make a big difference to you, or to a competitor? Is it an early warning signal of a change already under way? Then later you look back to see how good your judgment was. This process is a very powerful tool that I have seen many successful leaders use.

You may detect nothing for days and weeks, but such a practice will hone your perceptual acuity. Once you notice something, engage a friend about it: Did he see the same thing as you? BlackRock CEO Larry Fink is one of the world's most influential leaders of a financial institution, and his firm has more than twelve hundred investment profession- als. He told me that despite the detailed information he has at his fingertips, before going to bed he watches the world- wide news from multiple sources to detect the unexpected and check progress on things he thought would happen. He uses his highly honed mental faculties to see before others do, since part of his job and that of his leadership team is to consult with not only businesses but also the chairman of the Federal Reserve, the secretary of the treasury, and central bankers around the world. He is ahead of most in seeing sig- nals of change and thus in shaping the world.

Fink may spend twenty minutes viewing the news on his iPad, but because of his daily practice it takes him less than ten seconds to detect an oddity or contradiction and per- haps another twenty seconds to discern what it might mean. Through an e-mail that evening or in conversation the next morning he will compare his view with someone else's. If the CEO of this huge asset management firm can practice this tool, so can you. It takes just a small amount of time, but it can prepare you to shape and determine the destiny of your operation, business, or company.

Following are some anomalies to look for.

An accelerating trend. A trend by itself may be passive, but a change in its momentum can be, well, momentous. On December 3, 2013, *USA Today* reported: "From Thanksgiving Day through Cyber Monday online sales climbed 16.5 percent over the same period in 2012. Mobile devices accounted for more than 17 percent of Cyber Monday sales, up 55 percent from last year." Those numbers were higher than the experts expected and went hand in hand with sluggish brick-and-mortar retail sales. Gracia Martore, CEO of Gannett, *USA Today*'s parent company, at the time said she saw those numbers as a tipping point.

Another example of an accelerating trend involves both India and China. Immediately following Narendra Modi's election as prime minister of India in May 2014, the Chinese government took steps to intensify trade relations between the two countries, including an immediate visit by a high government official, followed by arrangements for subsequent visits by the premier and president of China in the near term. Any business leader in their trade flow needs to see these visits as a potential seed, imagining what the possibilities might be and watching for any actions, such as foreign direct investment by China or reduction of tariffs between the two countries, that may create new opportunities and accelerate economic relationships between the two countries.

Modi's trip to Japan in late August 2014 and his relationship with Shinzo Abe surprised many, including perhaps the Chinese government. He brought back with him the promise of $35 billion from the Japanese government and Japanese private enterprise to be invested in India over the coming five years in clearly defined industries like infrastructure and manufacturing. In addition, Modi announced that there would be a special team reporting directly to his office that included two Japanese citizens. This country-to-country investment arrangement is a first. Having India's foreign policy be heavily influenced by its economic policy is also a first. Early success will likely cause other nations, such as Taiwan, Singapore, and South Korea, to come to India.

An extraordinary event. Such an event need not be business related, but could be social or political. In May 2012 a director of Conoco Phillips discussed with me an issue he had been considering: whether to expand to India. He saw it as a tremendous opportunity but was concerned about the government of then prime minister Manmohan Singh, which appeared to be paralyzed by indecision. I suggested that he watch what would happen on July 19, 2012. He was puzzled by the specificity of the date until I explained that it was the day the new president of India would be elected. The outcome was far from clear at the moment, but there was speculation that Parnab Mukherjee might be the one. If so, he would be giving up his post as finance minister (he actually resigned from that position in late June 2012), and the choice of his replacement would make a difference. Indeed, the appointment of Palaniappan Chidambaram to this post was significant for India watchers. He had held the position twice before and was known for being highly competent and pro-reform. He in turn appointed Raghuram Rajan as new head of the Reserve Bank of India (India's equivalent of the US Federal Reserve). A well-known and influential economist from the University of Chicago and formerly chief economist and director of research at the International Monetary Fund, Rajan was a highly credible choice for this important job. This event pointed to the likelihood that a team of highly capable and reform-minded officials would work on the backlog of decisions, including providing clearer rules about foreign direct investment. It was the first time since India became an independent country that the two posts of finance minister and head of the Reserve Bank— the two most important positions for the Indian economy— would be filled by people who worked well together and had a close relationship. It was a sharp contrast from the war between the two previous incumbents.

In October 2012 Chidambaram took me out to dinner (arriving at the restaurant in a nondescript car) and in a four-hour discussion related to me how he had initiated interministry coordination to unclog the paralysis of decision making. Several of my major industrial contacts told me in December that licenses held up for years were now being approved. During Chidambaram's short tenure before the election of Modi, foreign direct investment began to flow again, and my clients were becoming cautiously optimistic. This is yet another example of the importance of perceptual acuity for spotting the seeds and the catalyst.

Potential scalability. Some college kids have come up with a device that could potentially make one of your best-selling products obsolete. Who could scale it up? What could the timing be? Create two or three scenarios in your mind. If you are practicing the art of being alert about early warning signals and who the catalysts are, you should be able to sketch the scenarios and their outcomes, opportunities, and breakthroughs quickly and consider what they would mean and to whom. Be sure to consider the possibility of speed: Apple's iPhone scaled up much faster than Nokia anticipated.

In mid-2014 Amazon was asking the Federal Aviation Administration (FAA) for permission to fly drones on its own property for research purposes. This was the latest act in CEO Jeff Bezos's obsession with fast delivery to individual customers. The learning is not just around his interest in drones, but also his insatiable curiosity about how to harness new technologies for the benefit of the consumer, and more specifically, his belief in the importance of speedy delivery. What are the implications for companies that are competing with Amazon now or might be in the future? Fast delivery means high velocity, or inventory turnover. An imaginative leader would want to know how quickly Amazon's research could produce a workable delivery system that the FAA could approve. But he would also want to keep an eye on India, which has not banned the use of unmanned aerial vehicles, and whose transportation system is woefully underdeveloped. Could Amazon's drones take hold very quickly and leapfrog the physical distribution infrastructure in some countries, the way mobile phones leapfrogged landline communications? Rumors are starting to circulate about test markets in Mumbai and Bangalore.[5]

Bezos bases his plans on what he believes will not change in the next five to ten years: customers' desire for selection, low prices, and fast delivery.[6] Even without drones Amazon has begun delivering merchandise in some US cities on the same day or even within one hour. If this faster delivery scales up, one thing it could do is create new opportunities in the packaged food industry, specifically for companies in the burgeoning health-food business. They could build a business model in a new market space: fast delivery of preservative-free products. It is an unmistakable signal for producers of health-conscious food products to be ready to scale up fast—and, of course, a threat to those who move too slowly or not at all. The concept of "shelf life" for a portion of the market could also be eliminated, since Amazon has no need for shelves at retail outlets, a game-changer for food companies and packagers.

Most forecasts are made by extrapolating from past data and identifying patterns through analytical techniques to predict future behavior. They may be helpful but are insufficient. Use the tools in the next chapter to be on the alert for what is new and different and imagine what the combinations and outcomes could be.

Many seeds of structural change make their first appearance as a challenge to a company's sales force or other frontline workers. It's not uncommon for a leader to see several quarters of declining sales and conclude that either his people are not executing well or a competitor is doing something better—ignoring this typical signal of a structural change in its industry or ecosystem. Then his or her successor is left to contend with the mess. As of this writing, for example, IBM's revenues have declined for three quarters in a row. Its senior management has cited an operational problem—the sales force is not doing its job—as the cause of the decline. But analysts who follow the company have a different hypothesis: that IBM is missing a major bend in the road. The market has changed. Customers no longer want to pay a high upfront investment to buy a licensed product for a fixed price; they prefer to pay for a product based on its usage and without having to make a fixed investment. This structural change began several years ago and has enormous implications for IBM's current management. In an industry moving at warp speed, simply reacting to these conditions won't be enough. IBM has superb technical talent, an embedded customer base, and an innovation machine. But its leadership seems to have missed in accurately perceiving what looks like a bend in the road for the company—or at least that's what some investors and analysts believe. As of this writing, some were calling for IBM to rethink its strategy, resource allocation, and focus to navigate this new bend in the road and build credibility with the skeptics. (Chapter 9 discusses how Adobe Systems recognized this market shift and successfully confronted a similar challenge.)

THERE ARE MANY ways to practice the skill of sorting, sifting, and selecting what matters from the vast and changing external landscape. Monsanto, for example, anchors its strategy in macro views of fluctuating global demand. The executive team and select members from senior operations stay in sync by meeting every four to five weeks to revisit the company's direction in light of external change. These executive team strategy sessions, held ten or eleven times a year, are held off-site so people can break away from the distractions of their daily work. They discuss what is changing not only in the competition but also anywhere in the value chain for food production, from fertilizers and farming to eating habits—and in the global geopolitical climate. The purposes are to hone people's antennae for picking up new trends, to generate new ideas, and importantly, to adjust the course.

These meetings and observations guided the company's recent move into precision agriculture. Monsanto leadership saw a unique opportunity to help farmers make more informed operational decisions by leveraging the company's deep data pools on seed research and combining it with information from increasingly precise equipment and other information. As a result, it made several acquisitions totaling more than $1 billion that brought together precision planting equipment, the big data analytics and modeling of The Climate Corporation, and other capabilities into one product platform by the close of 2014. By the end of the year, Monsanto's precision agriculture platform was giving growers actionable information on one out of every three acres of corn and soybeans in the United States with plans for premium services and expansion into other fast-growing agriculture markets like South America and Eastern Europe in future years.

Wherever you notice an anomaly, contradiction, or oddity, you need to imagine what the new landscape might be if what you're seeing is a signal of powerful change—and importantly, imagine how you might take advantage of the shift. Engage other people in your assessment. You'll expand your capacity to see the landscape from multiple angles, judge what's important, and speculate about how you could capitalize on it. You'll not only benefit from the diverse points of view, but also build your team's ability to detect change sooner—and be the next to create a bend in the road.

———

WE WILL CONTINUE to show how this skill can be developed in the next chapter by exploring additional tools for developing perceptual acuity.

CHAPTER 7

Tools to Build Perceptual Acuity

THE PRESSURES OF daily work and total immersion in tactical details can narrow your thinking and lower its altitude. "But what can I do?" you ask. "There are only so many hours in the day, and my job is at risk if I don't pay attention to operations and numbers in the here and now!" My response is that *practicing perceptual acuity is now part of your job* and will raise your value as a leader. And in fact, building it is less a matter of carving out time than of exercising the focus and discipline to watch and listen for different things in the ordinary course of your day. What follows are a range of tools you can choose from to develop perceptual acuity for yourself and your organization.

The Ten-Minute Exercise

Change doesn't wait for your annual planning cycle, so it's important to go through the process of trying to identify seeds and catalysts frequently. Some companies set aside ten minutes of each weekly staff meeting for that purpose. The rhythm conditions people to open their eyes and ears and gets multiple sets of radar working. Structural changes are often misdiagnosed as operating problems when they first surface, so it's a good idea to involve people at many levels of the company to help spot those changes.

In every staff meeting of an hour or more, devote the first ten minutes to learning about and discussing anomalies in the external landscape. Ask a different staff member at each meeting to present to the team a past, present, or possible structural uncertainty or bend in the road in another industry: What is it, why did it happen, or why could it happen? The person you ask to do this should rely on her own research using Google and other sources, not the views of consultants or other staff members. The team then discusses who is taking advantage of the bend in the road or the uncertainty, who is on the attack, and who is blindsided. This exercise widens the lens of the whole team and sharpens their antennae.

Staff meetings are usually held once a week, so the weekly drill of searching for seeds of radical change in areas people may not be familiar with expands everyone's viewpoints and helps them become more insightful. Most important is that it alters the attitude toward change and gives people permission to suggest changes in their own business. This is one of the most effective devices there is for personal growth and expansion of individual potential. And this practice becomes even more powerful when leaders at multiple levels lead such sessions with the people in their units. It can help the whole company become more externally focused and therefore less resistant to change.

Steve Schwarzman, the CEO of Blackstone Group, uses a form of this social tool at his Monday morning meetings. Blackstone is now one of the largest private equity firms, with businesses in several areas of the economy and more than $279 billion in assets under management as of the end of June 2014. Those attending Blackstone's staff meetings are connected on a daily basis to the highest levels of people in government, to investors, to leaders in diverse industries in countries around the world, and to sources of information about what is coming in the future. They are in the bridge of information. Schwarzman asks all attendees what is new, what they are detecting, and who the catalysts are. With a time lag of no more than a week, this group gains extensive knowledge about what is going on in the world, which in turn helps them contemplate what they can do to shape the game of their business and go on the attack. They are able to see structural uncertainties others may not, especially those tied to the inherent instability of the global financial system, giving them a heads up on what is happening before others.

Seek Contrary Viewpoints

Test your perceptions by talking with other people, especially those you expect might have opposite views. In one such discussion over lunch with some friends, I mentioned that I had been thinking about the business climate in China. The government had imposed fines on six makers of baby formula following an investigation of price fixing. I recalled that five years earlier, China had passed an anti-monopoly law designed to protect consumers and smaller manufacturers, and that one of its three pillars was to rein in abuse by dominant market players. Further, China's National Development and Reform Commission (NDRC), which had long been fairly hands off, had recently begun to staff up. I wondered aloud what those actions might mean for foreign companies doing business in China, including mergers and acquisitions, and we all began to imagine the future.

One person in the group immediately said: "It shows that the Chinese government is getting heavy handed. They can come after highly profitable businesses. I might not want to do business there because it won't be good for my share-holders." Another thought it would be wise to hire well-connected people in China if you were thinking of doing a merger, to try to complete it now before scrutiny intensified. But another chimed in with an opposite viewpoint: "Doesn't it show that the government is trying to do the right thing by preventing corruption or monopolistic behavior? Don't you think China is setting the stage for predictability and economic growth? Maybe President Xi is patterning China after the United States in the absence of an effective legal system, for the betterment of Chinese society. Isn't that a positive?" We were all looking at the same country, the same set of facts, yet we all saw things through different lenses. The discussion broadened our perspectives.

Tracking political events halfway around the world or emerging business models in other industries might seem beyond the scope of middle managers, but think again. The seeds of change that could make a company or industry ob-solete usually hit one product or market segment first. So middle managers should be honing their skill to develop in-sights about how the external environment is taking shape just as much as those in positions at a "higher altitude." And being close to the customer scene, as so many middle managers are, is an advantage in looking at the world through the eyes of customers. Middle managers are also in close contact with suppliers, and many have social networks in other industries, which are great sources for spotting new ideas. This skill will also help a middle manager make the case for additional resources, and on a more personal level, design a career path in tune with external realities.

Your social group, too, can sharpen your antennae. Surrounding yourself with people from different industries and backgrounds, with different cognitive bandwidths and attitudes about risk-taking, helps you see the same world through different lenses. Discussing your external perceptions lets you test them against theirs, so you have a better chance of being accurate. When "Clare," an executive in her midforties, became CEO of a company with $10 billion in revenue, she took the initiative to locate four other people about her age, also newly appointed as CEOs and running global businesses. Each CEO is in a different industry and has a different personal background. Each business is in a different sector of the economy: consumer products, Wall Street, information technology, and industry. They get together four times a year for dinner. Each group member also has access to varied insights from his or her diverse board of directors, direct reports, suppliers, and friends. Their meeting, and informal conversations between get-togethers, serve as a sounding board for each to cross-check thinking and provide a foundation for superb foresight. In addition, they all make it a habit to seek out and listen to people whose endeavors or expertise gives them insight into external change. They create a multiplier effect, magnifying each other's powers of observation.

Occasionally Dissect the Past

Another way to develop your perceptual acuity is on a historical basis. Here's where a glance at the rearview mirror can be helpful. Spend time with colleagues and look at a big external change that hit your industry or some other one sometime in the past fifty years. Dissect that change. What were its seeds, and who were the catalysts who caused the change? Take, for example, the shift to personal computers from mainframes, minicomputers, and word processors, which obliterated high flyers such as Wang Laboratories and Digital Equipment Corporation. Try to be specific about who and what caused that shift to happen—and why the losers failed to see the significance of what was happening. These kinds of discussions take time and mental energy, especially at first, but they are an important part of your work, and you'll get better and faster over time and be able to detect things sooner.

Dive into the Sources of Risk

GE has a global industrial imprint, garnering about two-thirds of its revenues outside the United States. It manufactures, sells, installs, and services its products in some countries with unstable governments that are geopolitically at risk. In contrast to many companies that seek to avoid risk, GE stipulates that risk is a part of its business model that should be managed, and that the company should be paid for the risk it takes in its business. This means that management must have rhythmic, disciplined mechanisms to detect signals of risk and take appropriate action ahead of others.

Steve Bolze, president of GE's power and water business unit, based in Schenectady, New York, operates in some fifty countries in areas considered high risk, such as many parts of Africa and the Middle East. The unit sells high-ticket items often costing hundreds of millions of dollars and representing long-term investments by customers. The lion's share of revenues, profits, and investments are non-US. To have an edge in managing the risk and taking advantage of the opportunities, Bolze receives regular summaries of select countries, highlighting key dynamics and implications. He makes a habit of studying these reports for early warning signals and catalysts. He also spends time with people in those countries, listening carefully. He explains, "We have some standard ways of gathering information and we use some external groups, but in terms of dealing with uncertainty, nothing substitutes for a personal visit. Having ongoing relationships with people in that country helps you understand the drivers there. Helping customers solve their problems also helps us understand the context. For example, five years ago we had to provide a significant amount of power to Kuwait. Meeting with the local government, partners, and the U.S. Embassy gave us a far deeper sense of when and how to move forward." His perceptual acuity is paying off: margins, market share, revenue growth, and cash generation are now the best in the industry. He and the power and water team are anticipating bends in the road and winning in risky areas.

Continually Build Your Mental Map of Changes in Multiple Industries

One day I was sitting at a lunch table during Microsoft's yearly CEO Summit with Warren Buffett and eight other people. As the discussion evolved, people expressed curiosity about what makes Warren so knowledgeable. What I learned is that Buffet reads some five hundred transcripts of investor calls each year, in which all the presenters state their views about their company and industry and what they anticipate in the future. Buffet's practice is to let people run the individual businesses of Berkshire Hathaway but watch for changes across industries that might prompt him to change the resource allocation in the portfolio. This is what makes him a great investor. Since Buffet has been practicing this for decades, his acuity has become highly honed to detect signals and catalysts that are over the horizon, an impressive skill given that his portfolio of businesses spans a significant portion of the national economy. In my observation, there is no one better at knowing the external context than Warren Buffet.

Consider Who Might Use an Invention, Patent, or New Law to Create a Bend in the Road

Is the inventor driven to make a difference? Is someone else likely to use the invention? Who has the interest and/or resources to do something with it? The declining cost and increasing capacity of microprocessors and the low cost of using the Internet were separate factors in the early 1990s, but Linus Torvalds saw a way to combine them to develop Linux through an open system network that tapped the brains of programmers worldwide. By spurring the creation of the free software platform, he was the catalyst who changed the destinies of some proprietary software and hardware producers such as IBM. IBM adopted it, and open systems are now routine.

Ask "What's New?"

When most people ask you "what's new?" it's an innocuous conversational gambit. But Jack Welch, the CEO of GE from 1981 to 2001, had a habit of trying to find out what really *was* new from the wide variety of people he met, and he perked up when he heard something fresh. In the early 1990s I had been working with executives at GE for more than a decade. One day at the Hyatt Regency in New Orleans I ran into Welch on an elevator. I said, "Good morning, Jack." He looked at me with his piercing eyes and said nothing. I offered the same friendly hello twice more, again with no response. Now I was getting anxious. Suddenly he asked: "What's new?" I shot back a three-word response to his two-word question—"zero working capital"—to which he responded, "Are you trying to sell me some consulting? Did you make it up? Who does it?" He was skeptical but not dismissive. When the elevator door opened he asked again who was using it, and I gave him the details about a CEO who was using the tool to make better use of his capital. It was a competitive advantage, since most manufacturing companies in those days used roughly twenty to forty cents of working capital to produce one dollar of revenue. The new approach freed up cash to invest in growth while at the same time improving customer satisfaction, since it enabled the company to make to order.

Welch called the CEO and took a business unit manager with him to spend several hours learning the details. He then sent his executives to visit the other company's plants, and they reported back that the system was real. Welch ultimately set a goal around zero working capital and initiated a course on it at Crotonville, GE's executive education institute. By the time Welch retired, this approach had saved GE several billion dollars in cash, which could be used to fund growth.

Now I teach the value of "what's new" in executive programs and in my coaching work with executives, and I get ongoing feedback on how effective this simple phrase is in stimulating new thinking, expanding the imagination, and connecting various insights.

I also make finding out "what's new" a daily habit. For example, in a recent discussion with an editor at the *Harvard Business Review* I asked what new topics he was interested in and which ones were presenting him with the greatest challenge. When he mentioned robotics I asked for more details; the response was that he didn't want to know about the way robotics will replace labor but what is over the horizon. I then connected the fact that Jeff Bezos at Amazon recently bought a robotics company, a critical ingredient in his business model of delivering merchandise in one day, with another piece of information: that Google has invested $500 million in buying a satellite company. Shortly thereafter I read in the *Economist* about the production and launch of very small satellites—no more than thirty centimeters—that were now in low orbit around Earth. These strands of information were seeds that could potentially be combined to create bends in the road for several industries, such as agriculture and transportation. I shared that insight with people in diverse industries around the globe who had asked me what I was observing. And it's important to note that this is not a one-way street; I learn from their observations as well. Since I meet different people in different industries every day, I get help building my acuity to see what uncertainties are taking shape and what bends in the road might be coming.

Different people have different ways of asking what's new. Jeff Immelt's habitual question is: "What do you think?" Another leader I know asks, "What's the most difficult thing you're experiencing?" A lengthier but more precise way to open discussions about what's new is by asking: What practices and underlying assumptions are common throughout our industry? Those commonalities are a source of systemic risk. One example is the remarkable similarity of mortgage lending practices before the financial crash of 2008–2009, when credit standards were uniformly lax. The overleveraged housing market was observable. If you see a buildup of some kind, consider what could light a fuse. Form scenarios of what might happen and watch for signals that something is taking further shape. Who could be the catalyst for a good change, or a bad one?

Use Outsiders to Multiply Your Capacity to Scan

Use third parties to search media across the globe and gather information on what critical topics are emerging and what anomalies are disrupting patterns. For example, a food company or an agricultural products company would be interested in issues related to genetically modified organisms (GMOs), the use of preservatives, and natural labeling. Scanning helps identify the new themes and patterns that are gaining momentum and from which quarters. The number of references in the press to GMOs has grown by a factor of thirty-eight since 1990, preservatives by a factor of eight, and natural labeling by a factor of thirteen. In one segment of the food business there is a direct correlation between concern about GMOs and a decline of total demand for its products in the United States. From this scanning a company should develop a way to deal with the trend defensively or offensively. Companies exist that provide such services.

Watch the Social Scene

Pay close attention to how society is changing and what new consumer behaviors are emerging. Social issues are picked up quickly by the media and are sometimes followed by increased scrutiny or regulation as they work their way into the political sphere. Clinical drug trials became a hot subject in India in 2012 when some political leaders noticed concern about the number of deaths among people who participated in the trials, even those from causes not directly tied to the drugs. The rhetoric escalated, accusations of corruption were hurled against some doctors, and activists filed a public interest lawsuit alleging the use by global companies of Indians as human guinea pigs. The public and political debate led to tough new rules being adopted in 2013, which squarely lay responsibility on the testing company for any injuries or deaths that occurred during the trials, regardless of cause. Momentum had built to the point where the government felt compelled to act quickly.

In the United States, enacting legislation can be a laboriously long process that starts with a lot of work by staffers. Knowing what issues are being discussed among staff and in various governmental committees can keep you on the alert. For new business models, look through the eyes of an investment banker and strategic planner. Read their reports or online journals to see what innovative models they're talking about, regardless of the industry.

Be a Voracious Reader

When reading books and publications such as the *Financial Times*, *New York Times*, *Wall Street Journal*, and *Economist*, look for what surprises you, what is an anomaly. My technique is to first read the roughly half-page "Lex" column on the last page of the first section of the *Financial Times*. Having read it for more than thirty years, I have found it to be very reliable on facts and insights. There are usually five items. I read Lex with a sense of curiosity about what is new, what I didn't know, and what might be the start of a trend. There may be days and weeks in which I find nothing. But when I do, I reflect on what it might mean and for whom. Who will be on the attack, who on the defensive, and why? Is there a game-changer here? Doing this with whatever you read will increase your ability to identify signals and catalysts that might create bends in the road. The special reports that appear every few weeks in the *Economist* provide great research on current topics from expert journalists who tap a wide variety of sources worldwide.

Here's a recent example of how one industry identified a signal and a catalyst and assessed their game-changing impact. In 2012 US automakers were recovering from the global financial meltdown and its aftermath. The domestic economy seemed to be over the hump, and rebounding consumer confidence, combined with low interest rates and the need to replace aging vehicles, was boosting year-over-year sales by double digits. Boards, investors, suppliers, dealers—everyone knows that the toughest competitors for the American automakers are the Japanese, so company executives tend to keep close track of what is happening in Japan.

This is what they picked up: in December 2012 Shinzo Abe became prime minster and clearly announced a platform to reflate the Japanese economy. He came into office with a strong political mandate to carry out his policy, because Japan had suffered miserably and lacked confidence after fifteen years of deflation and a stagnant economy. The US automakers' top brass saw that Abe was a catalyst and wondered what kinds of sparks he might ignite in Japan. It wasn't hard to guess that his economic policies might be aiming to increase exports and drastically lower the value of the yen to get Japan's engine running. Then again, talk is cheap. Moving past the rhetoric to get things done is difficult in any political scene, and therefore talk is easy to dismiss. Then came another catalyst: in February 2013 Abe appointed Haruhiko Kuroda as the new governor of Japan's central bank. Within two months Kuroda articulated and executed a policy to have the yen find a new value, which would boost exports from Japan. In five months, the yen found its new level, moving from 78 to 102 to the dollar. The US government welcomed the move, and from then on the yen stayed near 100.

From the time Abe was elected with broad support, the US auto leaders had roughly eight months to continue to think through various scenarios, revise their plans, and rehearse how competition might intensify in the coming years. The signal was clear that something would happen with the yen, and they should have imagined how deep a decline it might be and what the implications would be, for example, in the fight for market share or in matching price reductions. What would the competition from Japan do? What, then, should US automakers do about their resource allocation and new products? They should have been evaluating their whole business model, from pricing to product mix. Suppliers might be able to give a heads up: they would know if the Japanese automakers were gearing up to produce new models with higher value added, or if the suppliers were asked to increase production, which would mean the Japanese were gearing up their drive for market share. What the US automakers did do is travel to Washington to implore political leaders to include in their trade negotiations a stipulation that Japan not be allowed to manipulate its currency, a plea that fell on deaf ears. For me this is an especially persuasive illustration of how perceptual acuity, developed through practice, can at least give you lead time to adjust to external change—in this instance, triggered by geopolitical change.

THE NEXT CHAPTER describes three tools Tata Communications adopted to build the team's perceptual acuity.

CHAPTER 8

How Tata Communications Expands the Organization's Lens

PERCEPTUAL ACUITY HAS an especially high premium for industries such as telecom, in which fast-changing technologies and business models are in constant flux, and Vinod Kumar, managing director and CEO of Tata Communications, has been trying to institutionalize it. "One of the things we deal with all the time is rapid reconfiguration of supply chains and redistribution of profits among the various players within the chain," says Kumar. "We just have to make sure we're on the right side of the money-making equation." He knows there is no way to do that without a clear understanding of the big picture, so he has created mechanisms to build the organization's perceptual acuity.

The company, owned by India's $100 billion Tata Group, provides communication, computing, and collaboration infrastructure to large global companies to the tune of about $3 billion in annual revenues. Its optical cables connect continents and provide 20 percent of the world's Internet routers; it has a million square feet of data center and facilitates 35 percent of the world's roaming telephone traffic. Its customers fall into two camps: telephone companies and mobile operators—the Verizons of the world—and multinationals such as JPMorgan Chase, Pfizer, and Aetna, which need to link their distributed offices. The great complexity and uncertainty Tata's customers face is heaped on top of the high rate of innovation and change in its own competitive landscape. So while the company had a fairly rigorous three-year planning cycle, a longer range plan in the face of such change seemed almost meaningless.

Nonetheless, in early 2013 Kumar began thinking about extending the horizon. He decided to push beyond the usual conservative assumptions to see what the world might look like *ten* years out, and therefore what options might exist for "nonlinear growth." He convened his top team to make some projections unencumbered by current data, and the picture they conjured was one that far exceeded their current ambitions. Doing more of the same was not going to get them to where they imagined they could be; he had to get the organization oriented to a broader context so the team could identify the specific opportunities for growth.

It was clear that the kind of services Tata provides were in high demand, but that information alone offered little guidance. "We have to contend with rapidly declining prices in many segments," Kumar explained. "So providing services where we can also make a profit demands a lot of forward-looking thinking about what our business

can be—what size it could be, where the upside opportunities are, and what the potential risks might be." Customers
themselves were facing a lot of change in their business environment. Creating services they needed required understanding the worlds they lived in. As Kumar explained: "We
believed there was a huge opportunity to play a bigger role
instead of just being in the background. We felt we could
help customers succeed based on the changes that were taking place, by creating new services in education, media, and
entertainment, for example."

Kumar also believed that expanding its lens would help
the company pick up on new business models outside its industry. "Even if you're in our business—telecom or collaboration services—talking with knowledgeable people in other
industries such as pharmaceuticals invariably generates
ideas we can borrow, for example in terms of how to work a
supply chain. Many conversations don't lead anywhere, but
the time invested is worthwhile for those gems that generate
breakthrough ideas. There are very few conversations we can
have that won't inspire something that is actually relevant
to our business." Creating brand new segments or industries
was not out of the question. "If we could connect the dots
that were beginning to emerge, we could create completely
new sub industries or potentially even new industries over
time. We didn't know what those were yet."

Like those in any business, Tata's leaders were absorbed
by operational performance and getting better at managing
productivity and efficiency. They worked with what Kumar
likened to religious fervor to keep up on new developments
in their functions or technical areas in the face of increasingly short shelf lives for technology and cutthroat competition. To help reach a higher altitude and create a culture

of intellectual curiosity, of learning and exploration, Kumar took three specific actions: taking some of his top people to attend sessions at a highly renowned teaching organization, creating voluntary teams for exploratory projects they call "moonwalks," and formal training sessions designed to stimulate broader thinking.

In early November 2013 Kumar and a group of fifty-some leaders boarded planes and journeyed to San Francisco. Their ultimate destination was Singularity University, the institute founded in Silicon Valley in 2009 by two technologists—Peter Diamandis, a social entrepreneur known for founding the X Prize Foundation, and Ray Kurtzweil, a futurist and entrepreneur—to help business leaders and experts in various fields brainstorm how to harness technology to benefit society. The whole point at Singularity is what they call "exponential thinking." To achieve it, they set the bar ridiculously high, aiming, for example, at producing a vaccine for malaria that costs one cent per injection, or a solution to a problem that affects the lives of a billion people. Believing that the convergence of different technologies will sometimes lead to unexpected but highly powerful results, the faculty at Singularity are experts in a broad range of technologies: areas like neuroscience, nanotechnology, and robotics.

Especially considering the mutual interest in technology convergence, Kumar thought an executive program at Singularity was a good way to break the shackles of the mind created by the daily grind. With him for the one-week custom program were Tata Communications people from around the world and across functions, with others from a mix of backgrounds in taxes, human resources, product engineering, sales, and marketing.

The program was immersive, meaning the group moved seamlessly from one venue to another, from lectures to discussions to workshops. Thought leaders from around the world and tech leaders from Silicon Valley gave three- to four-hour presentations on topics such as artificial intelligence, machine learning, next-generation Internet, driverless cars, 3D printing for manufacturing and health care, and drone technology. Talks by former FBI agents about digital security and next-generation weapons were coupled with discussions of ethics and the morality of technology, in which provocative questions such as "What happens when a gun can be produced with a 3-D printer by a visitor to a country?" got the mental juices flowing.

Slowly people started to engage, think more broadly, and make connections between disparate trends, though not instantly and not everyone. Kumar had tried to prep the group for the session at Singularity by having outsiders come and talk to them. Enthusiasm was uneven in those get-togethers before the trip to San Francisco. "When you start this kind of journey, about a third of the people are sort of intellectually curious, and they get it," Kumar explained. "They say, 'Maybe there's something going on here.' Another third or so say, 'Okay, we trust you enough to think there may be some merit to it. Let's go along with the journey with an open mind.' Another third are sitting there saying, 'Hey, I have real business problems to solve. I have to meet this quarter's numbers, I have to improve a live process by 5 percent or I need to raise funding for a project.' They almost put up a wall."

Kumar didn't fight the holdouts. "I learned not to try too hard to persuade people that this was important. I planned the meetings, and they showed up. About a third of the people left Singularity University saying they still weren't sure how it was all going to pan out for us and what the relevance was, but one hundred percent of them said it opened their eyes to something they didn't know about. That outcome was a wow for me. A number of them said, for instance, that with all this technology that's emerging and the speed at which it is changing, they needed to have a discussion with their children about how this affects their lives and what they should be studying."

Following the session at Singularity, Kumar wrestled with how to fire up curiosity among a broader group of leaders, so he tweaked an existing mechanism. For several years Tata Communications had been using cross-functional teams to go off and solve an operating problem in 120 days. This approach had proven to be effective in making internal improvements and spotting talent. In 2013 it occurred to Kumar that the same technique could be used to broaden people's thinking. So Kumar chose some topics—artificial intelligence and machine learning, health care and biotech, additive manufacturing (3D printing), and alternative energy—and assigned a leader to each one. That person was to assemble a cross-functional team of ten or twenty volunteers from within the middle and senior management of the company. The assignment was open ended but clear: go and learn about the topic. Teams could do that any way they chose—by taking classes, doing research online, or engaging with academics or people from other companies. Kumar explained that the point was simply to go and explore: "There's no compulsion to identify the implications for us as a company. All you need to do is go learn about what's happening. What are the latest technologies, what are the trends, who are the emerging players?" After 120 days, the teams were to produce a white paper or video that captured the essence of the learning and could be shared with the top two hundred people in the company.

Kumar initially called this exercise "Future Gazing" but quickly changed it to "moonwalks," because, he explains, "I wanted to subtly say that this really is exploratory. We're going to walk on new terrains and hopefully find some useful nuggets." Enthusiasm for moonwalks grew, especially at the midlevel of the organization, and people started seeking them out. That interest encouraged senior leaders to carve out the couple of hours or so a week needed to keep them going. It also convinced Kumar to start another batch of teams when the first moonwalks were about a third of the way along. "There's no doubt in my mind that people will look at what they study in a very different light from what they were thinking before. It's all about making learning interesting again and reorienting people externally, not just to our industry and our competition but to other things that are happening on the outside. And I'm confident that it'll lead to things that will benefit us."

Tata's third initiative in 2013 was the launch of a more formalized training course, curated and taught by the leadership team using the case study method. Kumar himself teaches a module on the softer aspects of creative thinking, innovation, and external orientation. One exercise he conducted takes a business model or practice from another industry and brainstorms how it could be fitted to his industry. Most of the time it doesn't yield anything directly useful, Kumar says, but he sees value in taking a different perspective, because "It's training the mind to get out of the trap of linear thinking."

WHATEVER TOOLS YOU use to build your perceptual acuity, bear in mind that seeing the world through a wide lens is not merely an academic exercise. You need to use your observations to plot a course for your organization and steer it through the changes you detect. The next three chapters will help you define your path.

CHECKLIST FOR PART II

✓ Do you habitually pick up on anomalies, contradictions, and emerging trends by talking to people and reading newspapers and magazines?

✓ Have you expanded your information networks lately beyond your industry, country, and comfort zone in order to widen your lens and calibrate your thinking through other people's lenses?

✓ Do you have a routine mechanism for you and your team to pool your observations about the external landscape and to explore potential impacts on your business? Are you allotting sufficient time and attention to this?

✓ Have you identified catalysts whose activities you need to track? Have you identified the "seeds" that a catalyst could pounce on? Have you identified the barriers a catalyst would have to overcome to gain traction?

✓ Do you have a methodology for improving your perceptual acuity, such as forming hypotheses about a trend that might take shape or what a catalyst might do and revisiting your predictions later to see how accurate they were?

✓ Do you encourage and value perceptual acuity in those who report to you?

✓ What specific tools are you using to enhance your perceptual acuity and that of your direct reports? Have you developed a new tool?

PART III

GOING ON THE OFFENSE

CHAPTER 9

Defining the Path

PICTURE A HIGHWAY stretching more or less straight to the horizon. Yes, it has hills and bumps and curves, but as you look at it you get a pretty clear idea of the direction you're heading. That's life in the age of core competencies. Now imagine that the road takes a sudden sharp bend and branches off into a multitude of directions. Which way should you head? Will there be washouts or dead ends? This is the new world of leading in uncertainty.

Seizing the attacker's advantage is not the same thing as seeking new ways to use your core competencies. Rather, it is a process that starts with this central question: What new developments can I take advantage of to create a new need or give the customer or consumer a more compelling experience? Two things will greatly improve your ability to find a path through uncertainty: a sharp focus on the end-to-end experience of the customer or consumer and a working knowledge of digitization and analytics.[7]

Transitioning to a new path poses special challenges, but you can't let them stop you from defining where you need to go. Going on the offense is no longer optional, for one simple reason: defense alone means a shrinking business. Delivering the company's short-term bottom line and generating cash can backfire unless you find a new path. Activist shareholders sniff out companies that could divest a business or part of one that is not growing, or is not earning the cost of capital, or is more valuable to another company. You can try to fight the activists or fend them off, but unless you have a mind-set to pursue new opportunities, divesting just makes the company a bite-sized takeover target.

This is the situation that "Trico," a large manufacturer with businesses in three different industries, found itself in. To work their way out of low margin and high capital intensity businesses, the board recommended a hard-nosed portfolio analysis. First to go was a major division that represented 15 percent of total revenues. It consumed a lot of cash and had near zero growth. It was sold to a private equity firm. That left the core business and a smaller unit in a specialty niche. Activists started pressing the company to sell the smaller unit, which was making good money, growing, and producing cash, but, they argued, would be of more value to somebody else. Soon it, too, went on the auction block. Meanwhile the core business was getting a heavy dose of cost cutting, rationalizing, and geographic expansion. It had not yet established a new growth path. The company had reduced its capital intensity and was generating cash, making it a delectable takeover target.

Compare Trico's defensive posture with that of Adobe, the maker of software tools such as Photoshop and Adobe Reader, whose president and CEO, Shantanu Narayen, observed what he saw as a structural uncertainty on the horizon and went on the offense. In the first decade of the 2000s, cloud computing was newly emerging and not widely adopted, but Narayan saw how it nicely freed people from having to own expensive equipment and software applications. Instead they could essentially rent only the computing power they needed. Would cloud computing take hold? He reasoned that it would, that the desire to lower fixed costs would make it compelling to users. If that happened, Adobe's business model, whereby it licensed a software package to be downloaded to a device, would be out of sync with the direction the digital world would be going in. So Narayan began to contemplate how to reposition Adobe for this new "pay by the drink" computing era. Customers would no longer license and download software, he figured; instead, they would pay for a subscription and use it in the Cloud.

The prospect of a new business model raised difficult questions and challenges. It would be untenable to maintain two separate code bases, the existing one and one that would function in the Cloud, so Narayan would have to choose where to focus the company's energy and resources. Changing direction would have serious ramifications. For one thing, total revenue and the bottom line would temporarily shrink as the company spent money to build the new programming capabilities. And shifting to the Cloud would no doubt upset at least some members of his top team and the board, who were fully vested in the old model. Customers too might be unnerved. Of course investors would see all this and be very concerned if not outright skeptical about where Adobe was headed.

In the end, the decision to move quickly and ahead of other players to reposition Adobe for cloud computing won out over waiting for a massive industrywide shift. Narayan made a bet on the Cloud and helped his team see the urgency of the move. The transition was not easy, but as Adobe released its cloud-based products, the market responded far more enthusiastically than expected, and because Adobe was ahead of others, it was able to acquire small companies with the capability it needed before their prices were bid up. Investors have since rewarded Adobe for making a good offensive move.

I have previously stressed the importance of being agile and willing to change. You may have to change more than once if the path you initially chose turns out to be wrong. But you can't do it repeatedly, because this is more than a simple recalibration. Many parts of the organization and partners in your ecosystem have to be aligned with your strategic direction. Zigzags have a way of creating confusion and eroding trust among important constituencies.

At Yahoo, for instance, three CEOs in quick succession— Terry Semel, Jerry Yang, and Carol Bartz—each chose a path that led nowhere. The board had high hopes that Semel could turn Yahoo into a moneymaker. In one meeting I attended in New York around the time Semel was hired in 2001, Jerry Yang, a founder who was on the board until 2012, said that it took two years to get Semel to give up his post as chairman and co-CEO of Warner Brothers and come aboard. Semel positioned the company to get revenues from advertising, but the initial spurt in sales soon fizzled out. Yang took over but spent much of his energy fighting off an unfriendly takeover attempt by Microsoft, which he felt priced Yahoo too low. The failed bid sparked intense pressure from investors; as the stock price declined, talent began to leave. The board scrambled to find a new CEO who could set the course and win over the skeptics. They chose Carol Bartz, the hard-charging former CEO of Autodesk, who strode in with a focus on cost reduction and scale, striking a revenue-sharing deal to use Microsoft's search engine and share Yahoo's own search technology. Investors didn't buy in, and more talent left, including a key expert in search engines. By the time Yahoo hired Marissa Mayer, formerly of Google and widely celebrated as a rising business star, to be CEO in 2012, the company had lost ground to competitors in the fast changing market space. The organization was seriously demoralized. It's very difficult for a new CEO to chart a path in a short period of time. Mayer has been bold in making decisions and has a cash lifeline in Yahoo's holding of Alibaba stock, but the jury is still out. The frequent changes of direction have battered credibility inside and outside the company.

Consumers Hold the Key

Big data and algorithms can't completely replace an intuitive feel for the customer or consumer, which many top leaders lack. All too often other skills and traits win the bigger jobs, and soon you have executive suites totally out of touch with the human beings who actually use or consume their offerings. At some companies, promotion paths favor financial expertise over operating line experience, and immediate demands often squeeze out time that might be spent connecting with customers. Aggregate metrics are useful for control purposes, but are not particularly helpful by them-selves in understanding and reconceptualizing the total consumer experience or in defining options and deciding which to pursue. Big data can segregate buying behaviors, for example, but cannot show you how to segment markets and which ones to attack. The human mind is still unsur-passed at making connections to generate hypotheses that can then be tested and in many cases make the final judg-ment—or at dealing with unique situations that arise. UPS's ultra-sophisticated On-Road Integrated Optimization and Navigation system uses vehicle sensors, satellite mapping, and advanced algorithms comprising some eighty pages of code to recommend the best routes out of tens of thousands of alternatives. Yet there are instances when the drivers can override it. Says Jack Levis, who led the system's develop-ment, "We tell them: if the model has you doing something that won't meet a customer's demand, do what's right."[8]

The allure of something newer, better, or cheaper is what ultimately redraws markets and industries and shakes com-panies to their roots. "Better" means not just better than what you offered before but something that exceeds other avail-able options. Defining the path means figuring out what's missing from the consumer experience—or what could be a terrific new experience—and figuring out how you could fill the gap. What keeps things interesting is that consumer needs change faster than ever as technology allows instant online information sharing. At the same time, innovations and technology developments emerge equally fast, contin-ually generating potential new ways to meet those emerging needs. The "aha" moments come from observing both the external environment and the consumer and imagining the ultimate in convenience or cost from the consumer's perspective, using technology in some new way.

This kind of understanding about emerging consumer needs and their solutions takes holistic business thinking, playing with the various combinations of potentialities until something clicks. The insight might happen in a group discussion or simply when you wake up one morning with a crisp idea of where the business could go. This is what puts you on the offense.

In summer 2014 Harvey Koeppel, the former chief information officer (CIO) of Citigroup's global consumer group, told me how the idea for mobile banking was created. In 2003 he was visiting a recently created branch in Mumbai that had all the latest technology, and he saw how customers loved it. That night, at a long dinner attended by the head of Citigroup in India, Koeppel was fiddling with his Blackberry and the idea popped into his mind. He turned to the Indian manager and asked, "How would you like to have a Citigroup branch in a Blackberry device?" The manager replied, "Really? Can we do that?" Koeppel assured him that they could and proceeded to sketch out the application on the proverbial napkin. The venture was approved by headquarters, and the application was launched within three months. It was the first ever foray into mobile banking by any big bank.

You cannot develop an intuitive understanding of customers or consumers without direct observation. Even as CEO of Wal-Mart, Sam Walton walked the stores; countless others do the same. Steve Jobs's and Jeff Bezos's feel for the consumer, gained through keen observation, is legendary. Take another example, India's Kishore Biyani, founder and head of the highly successful Mumbai-based Future Group, with businesses in retail, brand management, real estate, and logistics. The company has its roots in retail, beginning with Pantaloons, a department store chain, and Big Bazaar, the country's leading hypermarket chain, sometimes referred to as the Wal-Mart of India. Biyani uses plenty of analysis to determine which markets and categories to enter and which to exit, but even in his elevated role he spends time to understand the consumer, and he makes it an organizational priority. "I'm on the floor twice a week and I take people with me," he says. "Wherever we go, we meet people. When we go to stores, we watch people, what are they putting in their shopping basket, who is making the purchase decision, what are they wearing, how are they behaving. We try to correlate our observations with what we build in that community.

"In our business, things change quickly. New products come about and get launched. We must be in touch with what's happening around us in society, and have an understanding of what influences that. Then we work through the data."

Retail outlets typically serve several communities, and the Future Group team does extensive research to understand the particular identities of each of those communities—not just their income, but also things like linguistic and religious differences, and whether they are migrants from other states in India, nonmigrants, professionals, and so forth. The team prepares detailed reports that explore why people behave as they do, whether they might change, and how well they would accept something new.

There is always a human observation behind the analysis. In late 2013 Biyani noticed that girls in some local villages were going to temple in jeans, which had always been taboo. He saw that shift as a sign of two things: a greater receptivity to Western clothing and more respect for girls. He thought, "If that change is now accepted, then other things will change as well. Society is shifting, and the family is allowing it." That observation had business implications. It meant that girls, and young people in general, might be more involved in purchase decisions. To prepare for that scenario, Biyani began to reimagine the company to include more young people, more women, and more people who understand diversity. "By 2015, we will have a different organization," Biyani said. The overarching lesson is that subtle differences in consumer behavior exist virtually everywhere. You need to pay close attention to them. Biyani captures the idea this way: "My job is to take decisions. If I don't understand customers, the organization could wither to nothing."

If you're a midlevel leader, you might have the kind of exposure to customers that will help you develop your instincts—but you can lose interest if you've been conditioned by a career's worth of reviews in which the boss obsesses over financial results and ideas are shot down if they're not backed by hard numbers. Don't let that happen. Visit customers and/or consumers regularly, make your own observations, and figure out how their needs are changing. That's how you'll develop your intuitive sense of evolving demand against the backdrop of the broader external changes, such as regulatory, geopolitical, societal, or technological. Focus in particular on the customer's pain points, and what might fix them.

The new challenge, in short, is to link your gut with a good enough understanding of digitization to imagine how you could use it to transform the consumer experience.

Your company touches the consumer in many ways, before and after the sale. How can technology, broadly defined, improve that end-to-end experience? Amazon is the go-to example—but remember that it was born of Jeff Bezos's personal enthusiasm for creating better consumer experiences. He was exposed early in his career to a brilliant mathematician named David E. Shaw, who started an investment company, D.E. Shaw, based on algorithms he had developed. Bezos saw what algorithms could do in finance. He was able to link that power with consumers' desire for a more efficient shopping experience. From then on, he saw ways to improve and expand the service, always working backward from the consumer experience to the sensors, algorithms, and software required to provide it.

Born and Reborn Digital

Companies such as Amazon that were born digital don't have to peel through layers of bureaucracy to become consumer centric. Nor do they have to integrate technology into their operations. They came into existence by combining a new technological capability with the leaders' sharp eye toward something the consumer needed but was missing. WhatsApp, bought by Facebook for $19 billion in February 2014, for example, met the need for instant messaging while protecting the user's privacy. The most successful of this born-digital breed can scale up incredibly fast. Capital is readily available to them, and their business models are inherently light on capital intensity and cost. WhatsApp had fewer than fifty employees when it was acquired.

Adapting to digitization, let alone capitalizing on it, is a different story for legacy companies. Big corporations have tens or hundreds of thousands of employees and huge investments in physical plants and equipment. Their technology investments enhance or replace physical activities, but rarely is digitization at the core of their business. This is a huge inhibitor of going on the offense and leaves the door open for a born-digital company to swoop in and use new capabilities such as the Cloud, advanced software, algorithms, and big data to improve the customer experience, putting high-margin segments under attack.

Legacy companies must think about how to harness digitization in any or all of its forms to provide better information about the consumer and to create new and better experiences. As GE's Steve Bolze puts it, "All of us as leaders need to get up to speed on big data and analytics and how to use them. Everybody has to kind of go back to school." (He did so by spending time with GE's Industrial Internet unit in San Ramon, California.) As you imagine the possibilities, don't immediately try to nail down the particulars of how your company will transition to a new trajectory or make the necessary investments. Think first about how digitization allows you to create something new and compelling and stay focused on the customer or consumer.

Companies can be reborn digital if their leaders have a mind-set for offense and the courage to venture into uncharted waters. Consider the direction Macy's is taking toward becoming an "omni-channel" retailer, blending store, online, and mobile by investing in technology over the past five years to improve the shopping experience and learn about its customers. Its path is based partly on existing technological capabilities and partly on the insight that consumers use a mix of media to shop for, compare, buy, and return merchandise. A woman might compare dresses online, try one on at the store, order it online, and return it in person, for instance. For some items, she might prefer home delivery. Algorithms help determine whether to pull inventory from a fulfillment center or a nearby store. Chief Financial Officer Karen Hoguet says: "It's not just that consumers need the goods right away. It is more about being on the cutting edge of technology."[9] Some products have radio frequency tracking devices to provide information that helps improve displays and sales. Macy's is also testing location-based technologies to push targeted offers to consumers while they are shopping in stores. Can retailers remain purely bricks and mortar? Some will, although they may be repurposed, but that must be a deliberate choice and not a default position for lack of knowledge or courage to act.

Be decisive if you choose to make the shift; if you vacillate, a born-digital player will move swiftly to capture your juiciest, most profitable segments. If that player gets hold of them, your decline will be swift, because it will constrict your blood supply—namely cash—and the loss of customers will accelerate.

Using Math for Offense in Health Care

Leaders who are on the attack find ways for their companies to be reborn digital when the opportunity presents itself. In health care, the Affordable Care Act is sharply accelerating trends already under way, causing uncertainty throughout the chain of the dysfunctional $2 trillion plus US health-care industry—and opening huge growth opportunities for those who adapt. Every player—from primary care physicians, to health-care providers such as hospitals and clinics, to the health insurance intermediaries and suppliers of IT systems—will be affected. For example, health-care providers that are paid a fixed fee to manage a patient's health will end up managing the risk, not the insurance company— a major structural change that will redefine the reason for the insurers' very existence. Similarly, providers have been paid on the basis of the services they rendered to a patient. The fee-for-service model will shift to some form of fixed price or contract per patient or community. The likely outcome is a far more effective and efficient health-care system, in which consumers will become increasingly empowered to take responsibility for their own health-care choices. In fact, it should boast many of the features that reformers have long been calling for in vain—brought into being not by policy fiat but through sound market principles.

Companies that are aggressively adopting the use of mathematics will help to shape the industry transformation rather than becoming victims of it. A unit of Novartis, for example, is collaborating with Google to develop contact lenses that can be used to monitor a person's health. Other companies are experimenting with wristbands, smart phones, and other forms of portable technology that monitor health as part of a patient's preventive care.

UnityPoint Health, based in Des Moines, Iowa, is developing an imaginative new business model based on mathematics. A UnityPoint patient has a unique relationship with a physician-led team of health-care providers in the organization, with access on a 24/7 basis. The relationship is based on trust and the ability to communicate, and the nurse is a crucial point of contact. The company is investing talent and funds to build an infrastructure of digitization, algorithms, and software that integrates aspects of patient care from various departments: pathology, MRI, and so forth. Centralized collection and analysis of data can help UnityPoint improve therapeutic treatment. The nurse and other providers have instant access to information from the patient and other sources, including the patient's adherence to the treatment regimen and progress. Simultaneously, the company is upgrading the nurses' skills and training to manage the fixed price contract the patient has with the company. Bill Leaver, the CEO of UnityPoint Health, even foresees an information-driven future in which patients need not always visit a facility to receive care.

———

EVEN THE BEST strategic thinkers can be weak on offense if they lack the courage to move in the face of uncertainty. The next chapter will help you see what psychological blockages might be holding you back.

CHAPTER 10

A Mind-set for Offense

BESIDES THE MENTAL gymnastics described in the previous chapter, setting a clear path in the face of uncertainty includes a psychological component. Your tolerance for ambiguity and risk will be tested, because going on the offense almost always requires taking action before you have a crystal clear picture of all the factors your success will depend on. You must be willing to commit to a new path forward even when some things are fuzzy, knowing that you will adjust your path along the way. This is the mind-set of offense for moving ahead and creating uncertainty for others.

As CEO of Thomson Corporation (now Thomson Reuters), Dick Harrington was a broad thinker with a finely tuned antenna for picking up signals about the outside world. He had a habit of talking to a lot of people, some inside the company, some not, and asking a lot of questions. In the late 1990s he and two men he had been conferring with—John Doty, a trusted advisor to the Thomson family, and Geoff Beattie, who ran the Thomson family fund that owned the Thomson Corporation—noticed a couple of trends beginning to take shape. As they began to think through how those trends might impact Thomson's business as a publisher of regional newspapers and professional journals in the United States and Canada, Harrington became uneasy.

Browsers had undergone fast development in the 1990s and by the middle of that decade were taming the Internet, making it much easier for nontechies to use. As a result, Internet usage was rising; from 1995 to 1998, the percentage of US adults using the Internet jumped from 10 to 36 percent. Would people really stop reading newspapers and journals? Nobody knew for sure, or to what degree. Even if they continued to read newspapers, what about the underpinnings of Thomson's business model? The bulk of revenues was from sales of classified ads and display ads. Could classified advertising, which accounted for half of Thomson's bottom line, shift to the Internet in a big way? At the same time, the retail landscape was changing. National chains such as Gap and Target were putting the squeeze on regional department stores, and to cut costs, the regional players were trimming back their budgets for display ads in newspapers. The national chains were not exactly taking up the slack. They preferred to use circulars inserted into newspapers rather than display ads, and these were less profitable for Thomson.

Thomson was stable, profitable, and still performing well when Harrington concluded that the forces affecting its sources of revenue would not reverse. And while other media companies lamented the changes in their industry, Harrington went on the offense. He formed a view about how the potentialities could combine so that Thomson could create value by expanding into information services delivered electronically, using the company's existing professional and specialty publications as a base. With storm clouds still far on the horizon, Thomson prepared to exit newspapers altogether.

Before moving forward, Harrington had to win the owners over to his point of view and his plan to build a future for the company. That included the daunting task of persuading Lord Thomson to give up what was at the time the world's largest newspaper chain. To the credit of his own inclination for offense, Lord Thomson understood what Harrington and the others saw and backed the plan.

A defensive mind would have seen gloom and doom in the rise of electronic media and might have sought to buttress the print business. Harrington's mind-set for offense saw the opportunity to build a business based on something new. He won support, and he and his team spent the next several years transitioning the business, including spending $7 billion to acquire more than two hundred businesses that met Thomson's new strategic and financial goals. They moved confidently to integrate them into a whole and convert the print businesses to digitization. The mind-set to not only recognize the new realities but also use them to advantage put the company onto a new trajectory ahead of others.

Competitors have not fared as well: some went on an acquisition spree and heaped up debt, Knight Ridder no longer exists, and others struggle to keep their newspapers profitable. In 2013 the CEO of a US-based newspaper chain revealingly said, "Our mindset is stuck in print, not digital." That comment came just before the company undertook a major restructuring that redirected resources to a higher growth path. Even the venerable *New York Times* seems to have suffered a decline. In May 2014 a ninety-six-page report prepared by an internal committee at the *Times* painted a dire picture of that newspaper's standing vis-à-vis digital publishing. The report, leaked to the Internet and posted on the Scribd Web site, found that technical and organizational weaknesses—for example, keeping technology and editorial siloed and doing a poor job of optimizing search engine results—were putting the esteemed publication at a disadvantage against players such as Huffington Post that had not earned the stature and respect of the *Times* but were savvy about digital media.

Playing offense doesn't mean you have to be the very first in a segment. The world doesn't change the day a technology is invented; for example, search algorithms were being developed for years before Larry Page and Sergey Brin created Google. Your specific timing depends on your assessment of how the market space is evolving and being reshaped, your resources, your need for partners and alliances, and your own and the company's ability to withstand setbacks and failure (and, of course, the strength of your concept). Your position may be good enough to let momentum build before you act. In some cases the new market is expanding and being resegmented, leaving plenty of room to grow without having to fight for someone else's share. In that case, patience can serve you well while you monitor the seeds and catalysts and gather the right competencies, resources, and partners. As we saw previously, GE under Jeff Immelt's leadership is making a big push on the Industrial Internet to speed the integration of algorithms, software, and sensors connecting complex equipment. Given the immensity of this burgeoning new field, GE has plenty of room to enlarge its share of the expanding market, and by building scale fast, it is reshaping the landscape.

Beware, however, that you don't confuse patience with a frustrated desire for certainty. Leaders often delude themselves when they say "let's let the market develop," assuming their company will have the strength to jump into the new area and dominate it at some point in the future. That's how Barnes & Noble lost so much ground to Amazon; it has shrunk and continues to shrink. Sometimes a clearer picture comes too late.

Removing the Blockages

Even if you educate yourself about digitization and the consumer, your own psychology may get in the way of finding a path to take advantage of uncertainty. Paying keen attention to the deeply rooted subconscious blockages—your own as well as your team's—will help transform your mind-set from defense to offense.

For example, a recent personal experience shows how deep those psychological barriers can be. The twenty most critical senior executives of "Tiptop Snacks" convened from around the world during the spring of 2014 to discuss corporate strategy. Tiptop Snacks was the industry leader, but "Gail Jones," the CEO, was worried about the accelerating shrinkage of the sweets market, the company's mainstay, and wanted to poll the team for ideas about where the maker of snack foods could go from where it was. Contention for market share against its toughest rival was getting ugly. Wall Street and the media, fixated on any deviation in volume and quarterly earnings, were relentlessly making comparisons. The demands of tight margins and cutthroat competition left the leaders of Tiptop Snacks little time to think creatively. Jones invited me to help her team open their imaginations so that they could visualize the evolving forces that were reshaping the market space.

I started by soliciting their views about what they saw happening in the external landscape. "Don't worry about how it pertains to your business," I said. "Just talk about big shifts or trends you've seen in industries that have been eliminated or are on the decline."

It was a struggle for most of them. One person outlined the erosion of their market share; another described inconsistencies in the brand; still another commented on macroeconomic issues that were affecting the demand for their product overseas. No one seemed able to cut the cord with the day-to-day business or to think beyond the boundaries of their industry. So I tried a different tack. "Let's look at digitization," I suggested. "What do you see happening there? What are some new developments emerging, and who is benefiting from them?" As we kept talking, more of them became engaged, and they quickly created the usual short list of game-changers: Amazon, Google, and Facebook. But when I took one of those companies and asked the group what bend in the road such a company could create next, and for whom, there was an awkward silence.

Eventually we dug into several of the game-changers and discussed how they had already affected other companies. Then we talked about a few companies that had completely missed the bend in the road, and why that might have happened. I asked the "why" question five times. Why did the company do what it did? And *who* is the company—that is, who are the key leaders, and why did they do what they did? We were making progress. Or so I thought, until I saw the notes that were circulated after the meeting. In trying to encapsulate thoughts about the external environment, the summary the team prepared reverted back to focusing on their market share, competition, and margins.

Jones reconvened the group every eight weeks and kept putting the bigger picture in front of the team. The more time they spent on the external context, the more they realized the urgency of shifting their focus to finding new paths. But there were some holdouts. The boundaries of their thinking had been compressed through years of focusing on the immediate issues within their clearly defined industry. As months passed and three team members continued to struggle to see the bigger picture, Jones realized that she couldn't wait. Their inability to see beyond the dynamics within the existing industry was slowing progress in going on the offense, and speed mattered.

These were great people, but they were becoming blockages. As painful as it was, Jones had no choice but to move them out of their jobs. Meanwhile, she prepared for the possibility of another blockage: two highly influential, long-serving board members were likely to have the same trouble shifting their perspective. She could remove the people who reported to her, but she could not change the directors. She would have to work intensely to communicate with and enlist the help of the other directors to bring their colleagues around.

Even with good intentions and a sense of urgency, going on the offense in the face of uncertainty is a stretch for many people. If you can't see a path, don't kick yourself. Accept that you may have to overcome years of nose-to-the-grindstone habit that has you subconsciously filtering out changes that will make your existing business the ham in the sandwich and limits your imagination about how to reshape the business. Following are some of the blockages I have seen interfering with people's observational acuity and decision making:

- Attachment to your existing core competencies
- Inability to build a new core competency
- Obsolescence of key people
- Fear
- Avoidance of opposition

Attachment to your existing core competencies. Many will lock onto these with a death grip, on the assumption that they are its greatest or perhaps only strength and its foundation for a secure future. After all, they are the source of the company's high margins, market share, and profitability. Especially if you helped build the competencies that have been the basis of success, it's hard to see that they may be becoming irrelevant in the changing landscape. The CEO of Kodak is the poster child for this problem: he focused on geographic expansion into China, building on Kodak's great expertise in film photography, and despite his background in semiconductors, missed the implications of the shift to digital photography. John Akers, IBM's CEO in the early 1990s, was locked on its core competency in mainframe computers. His successor, Lou Gerstner, liberated the company from that blockage and refocused it from hardware to software and services, where the new game was emerging. And it's not just the competencies themselves that can entrap you. Often relationships with suppliers and distributors that you have cultivated over many years and that have been key to your success make some topics of discussion taboo. A strong interconnection between Intel and Microsoft, which built such a strong PC franchise across the globe, seems to have contributed to both players missing the move to mobile phones.

Inability to build a new core competency. If you don't believe you can break with the past or muster the resources to do so, you will tend to cling to your existing strength, maybe with some minor tweaks. Many leaders lack experience building new competencies, or imagine that it can't be done. Yet that is precisely how some large-scale entrepreneurs succeed. One such is GMR, the largest infrastructure company in India. Based in Bangalore, GMR has grown to $10 billion in revenues largely by entering businesses it knew nothing about and building competencies in them. Its strength had been in banking, but its leaders saw much greater opportunities in building and operating power plants and later airports. They are no longer in the banking business; instead, they positioned themselves to grow with India's economic expansion. The new path has not been smooth: in 2012 GMR got into a cash bind, because of the uncertainties caused by the Indian government. Muddled policies squeezed the availability of coal and gas, and the government delayed payments for operating airports. Having learned the risks of depending heavily on government, GMR's leaders are again searching for new opportunities to grow—but confident that the disciplined methodology they have developed will enable them to build whatever new core competencies they will need.

Obsolescence of key people. Sometimes you subconsciously dismiss new paths before you even explore them because you know that the people you have depended on most don't have the experience or expertise to pursue them. For example, a traditional consumer products company may have to become a math house and develop capabilities in the use of algorithms. If you don't acquire that expertise and deploy it quickly enough, you may be limiting your company's future. Combine that with paralyzing discomfort about replacing people who have served well in the past with new high-priced experts, and you have a formula for eventual decline. No one wants to abandon people who have helped them succeed, but if that sentiment stops you from having a clear view of where the business should go, by definition it's a blockage. A variation on this theme is the delusion that a key person will change. People can and do learn. The question is, can they change fast enough? Gail Jones faced up to the hard reality that some could not.

Blockages about people have to be tackled directly; they can't be allowed to cloud your thinking. Zee Entertainment Enterprises, one of India's largest media and entertainment companies, began recruiting "digital natives" and having them participate in decision making at the highest organizational level side by side with executives whose careers were built in an analog world. That move ruffled some feathers, but Chairman Subhash Chandra wanted to make the change before his company became obsolete. As he put it, "We want life before death, not life after death." He is on the offense.

Fear. Despite the unwavering confidence business leaders outwardly display, many have psychological blockages rooted in fear: of being shown to be wrong, of being embarrassed, of how others will respond to their decisions or actions, and more generally, of the unknown. Uncertainty dishes out heaping doses of such emotion.

To be sure, fear can be constructive at times. In his book *Only the Paranoid Survive* Intel founder and former CEO

Andy Grove made the point that a heightened awareness of your potential doom—what Grove calls the "strategic inflection point" that will upend your industry, not just your company—can open your mind and build your courage. But if you let subconscious fears block your judgment, you won't know how to gauge the degree of business risk. Going on the offense does not grant you permission to gamble a business on hunches or theories for which the possible consequences are not thought through, but it *does* involve risk-taking. Becoming aware of and confronting your inner fears will allow you to see things more accurately, think more creatively, and move more decisively.

I often travel to India and other emerging markets, where laws and regulations can change very abruptly. For example, beginning in the early 2000s there were indications that the Indian government would allow foreign insurers to raise their ownership stakes in Indian companies from 26 to 49 percent, and firms made plans accordingly. But as that 26 percent cap persisted, some foreign firms such as New York Life pulled out. Then in 2014 Finance Minister Arun Jaitley announced that the cap would increase to 49 percent after all. Meanwhile, in March 2013 India's Insurance Regulatory and Development Authority (IRDA) issued tough new rules affecting such things as product design and policy payouts, and the insurers had a short six months in which to rethink their strategies. And in an unrelated sudden move, the Indian legislature hastily voted to impose a retrospective multi-billion-dollar tax on telecom company Vodafone after India's Supreme Court ruled in Vodafone's favor on the tax charge. That action caused foreign direct investment to all but dry up. It's easy to see why the prospect of such surprises can fill people with anxiety and fear.

Some leaders are psychologically able to cope with the unpredictability without becoming fearful. "It increases the tenacity of the leadership team to be agile and responsive to these changes on a minute to minute basis," says Analjit Singh, chair of Vodafone and founder and chairman of Max India Limited, a billion-dollar-plus conglomerate based in New Delhi that includes an insurance business. "I am not unlike other leaders in my part of the world in this way. We are accustomed to these things. I have spent a lot of time in the United States, and I know it is a very hard working country. It's hard to find an executive who has taken ten to fifteen days off a year. But we are alert every second. While America is on its feet, we are on our toes."

Trying to ignore uncertainty only increases fear, triggering a variety of symptoms, from withdrawal or losing control of your temper to suppressing bad news and blaming others. Dean Stamoulis, who heads global leadership and succession services for executive search firm Russell Reynolds Associates, observes that such fears and insecurities often take the form of a victim mentality. "Blaming and rationalizing is an extreme red flag," he notes. "I'm passionate on the point that the best senior executives I've seen have no evidence of whining. They take personal ownership for dealing with the situation they face, which shows a level of accountability and confidence in themselves to figure it out. That's what's needed in highly uncertain, ambiguous situations. Blaming indicates a thinking style that is not effective in uncertainty, and it erodes the connection with whatever constituencies are taking the heat."

Here's the message: become conscious of your blockages and embrace uncertainty. The more you dive into it, try to see its sources, and form a viewpoint about it that you can test with other people, the more conviction and confidence you will gain—and you'll be energized by it.

Avoidance of opposition. The blockage I've seen most often is the one that comes from the desire to avoid pushback and resentment when you press for major change. If you're in a turnaround situation and a business unit is losing money, you might cut it loose, and while some people won't like it, they're not likely to challenge the basis of your decision. But if you see something shaping up on the horizon that others don't yet see, and you want to shift focus and resources to pursue it, you're going to raise some hackles with your bosses in the hierarchy and your team—and if you're CEO, with the board, investors, and maybe a few powerful direct reports. If you doubt your ability to bring such powerful people along, you could rein in your ideas.

This concern is not unfounded. When you push for a radical change but have a weak power base and/or a strong internal competitor, you clearly do run the risk of triggering a backlash or a revolt. I've seen this happen in the executive suite a number of times. In one instance a chief operating officer (COO) who opposed the CEO's strategic direction sat in the weeds for a while, the whole time building his relationship with the board, then began making his dissatisfaction known and proposing an alternative path. One morning the CEO met with the board, and upon leaving the room, announced his resignation. The COO became the next chief executive.

You can ease your concern by getting other people on your side: bosses, employees, investors, the board, and outside constituents. You can win them over by helping them develop a mind-set for offense along with yours. In an organization of any size, a small number of people—some 2 percent—have a disproportionate influence on the other 98 percent; I call this the rule of 98–2. Never lose sight of the 2 percent. Their buy-in will make a difference in what signals get picked up, what new ideas get floated or nixed, and speed. Make a practice of tapping their observations and sharing yours, and make the path concrete by translating it into specific priorities and actions. If you're the CEO, talk to the board and the investment community to help them see what you see. That will create a frame of reference and build trust. The same approach applies to middle managers, who can bring their bosses along.

Where Courage Comes From

Becoming aware of your psychological blockages and working incessantly to overcome them will free your thinking to conceive a new path, but ultimately, this is a test of your courage. Do you have the guts to make a big move? Intellectualizing is one thing; having the courage to pull the trigger is another. "Savoring complexity and processing it intellectually is a learned skill that needs to be well developed," says Stamoulis. "But the capacity to act is a reflection of self-confidence—not behavioral boldness or arrogance but genuine authentic self-confidence about one's ability to figure things out and deal with the consequences. That self-confidence is vitally important when the unexpected occurs."

You have to harden your inner core to see the world as objectively as possible, think things through carefully, and act on what you see. You can't be a wimp. Carl Hahn, CEO of Volkswagen (VW) in the 1980s, was the maverick who expanded into nascent markets like China, Poland, and Mexico and built manufacturing and organizational capacity to capture customers there. His move was widely criticized at the time, and he was later dismissed, but he was prescient: today VW is the number one automaker in the world, and China and Mexico are jewels for the company.

You can never completely eliminate uncertainty. Doing nothing can be risky in itself, and there will always be some unknown unknowns—risks you don't even know exist despite careful thinking. But pinpointing the particular signals that your assumptions were right or wrong can build your confidence to step onto the path. You'll feel better knowing there's a way to judge how fast to move and when to adjust or abandon the path altogether.

Imagine, for example, that you are in the retail banking business and are immersing yourself in the uncertainties of mobile payments. You've been earning a high percentage of profits from credit cards, going toe-to-toe for years against a handful of known competitors in an established ecosystem of customers, credit card issuers, merchants, and transaction processors. But now the Internet and smart phones are everywhere, and people are using them for everything. In places like Africa, where banking infrastructure barely exists, mobile phones take the place of brick-and-mortar banks. In advanced countries, companies like PayPal have sprung up to facilitate online shopping, and others like Square turn mobile phones into electronic wallets. New players have proliferated and are in a perpetual do-si-do, moving from one category to another. PayPal is now an issuer of credit, along with Bank of America, Citigroup, and US Bank. Square is a provider of electronic wallets competing with Google,

PayPal, Softcard, and MasterPass; it is also a point-of-sale vendor, as are Verifone, Igenico, NCR, and Shopkeep. Mobile wallet hardware vendors include Apple, Samsung, Sony, Broadcom, and Telecom Italia. Now Amazon has jumped into the fray, and no doubt others will also.

This is enough information to conclude that the credit card business will be facing structural uncertainty for some time to come. Will the hardware-based players like banks have an edge in influencing the adoption of digital wallets, or will the players who host their payment systems in the Cloud gain the advantage? Will consumers like the variety of choices or find it bewildering? Will certain solutions emerge as best of breed, forcing consolidation? Will something called a credit card even exist in the future, or will all transactions be electronic? Can companies that are reborn digital even hope to win against those that are born digital?

To tame the uncertainty, you will need to define the questions that need answering and the factors to watch to get your answers. If it's important to know whether the mobile payments landscape will be fragmented or consolidated, consider what will make it go one way or the other. Watch to see if the variety of offerings creates confusion or hassles for the consumer, and whether companies are therefore trying to coordinate better. Or does the variation give consumers a customized experience they like? These trends are observable by watching consumer behavior and will give you a heads up. Similarly, to know if mobile payments will be hardware or cloud based, consider an influential factor like data security. Are technologies developing to protect consumer information in the Cloud, or are massive security breaches eroding consumers' confidence? It's perhaps notable that when it introduced its ApplePay mobile wallet in September 2014, Apple had already lined up an emerging ecosystem of some 220,000 retailer participants, including Whole Foods, Nike, and Walgreens, and included a fingerprint sensor. What security measures might develop next?

LEGO Group offers an instructive example of gaining confidence by pinpointing what you don't know, particularly about the consumer experience. In 2012 the Danish toymaker planned a major expansion into Asia, but as CEO Jørgen Vig Knudstorp and his team discussed the specifics of their expansion plan, they kept unearthing questions that had no clear answers.[10] Waiting for clarity was not an option, so they immersed themselves in the uncertainties they were facing to better understand them. The uncertainties fell into three broad categories: how the products would be received in the marketplace, how to sell and distribute products, and government regulation. They then divided themselves into three groups to probe each of these areas in depth and create options for how things might go.

One unanswered question was whether Asian consumers would care about the brand. LEGO is a well-known, high-quality product in much of the world, but it was relatively unknown in Asia. Maybe Chinese consumers would see plastic bricks as a commodity and shop only by price. Also unclear was how to market the product. LEGO was typically seen as having educational value, making it popular with parents. But research was showing that while Asian parents valued education, they expected toys to be a fun diversion. Many LEGO products are also built around themes tied to new movie releases. The success of those tie-ins varied greatly—as much as 30 percent—from one local market to another. Would global themes succeed in China?

How LEGO would sell and distribute the product opened another can of worms. Small retailers were still dominant in China, but big box retailers were making inroads. Which would prevail? Small retailers cared about profit margin above all else, while big retailers wanted inventory management and turnover. The biggest question about regulation was whether there would be commonality among countries or multiple sets of rules to comply with. Vietnam had a rule about the percentage of slack space in packaging, for example, which required a redesign specifically for that country.

Isolating the unanswered questions and gauging the speed with which they were likely to go one way or another became a guide to management. The team adopted a "watch and see" approach to some slow-moving, low likelihood possibilities, such as the loss of premium pricing power. But they needed to move fast on the question of where to manufacture and what to do if LEGO ultimately flopped in China. The answer was to create a manufacturing platform that had flexibility built in and at the same time to develop a process for exiting products expediently. To deal with the uncertainties of market acceptance, the company committed to do more granular research and to hire more locals. In the end, the willingness to wrestle with the uncertainties it faced made the company more attuned to them and better prepared to deal with them.

———

AS WE HAVE SEEN, your mind-set is not a given. It can change, opening the mental pathways to see opportunities in uncertainty. The next chapter describes how George Halvorson, as CEO of Kaiser Permanente (he has since retired), did just that, going on the offense despite the tremendous uncertainty in health care.

CHAPTER 11

Kaiser Permanente's Path Through the Turmoil in Health Care

YOU DIDN'T HAVE to be a genius in the early 2000s to sense that health care was going to change, but how dramatically, in what ways, and what the implications were for various participants was as opaque as a brick. The entire industry—a mix of very large players such as hospital chains and insurance companies (as large as $80 billion in revenue) and small players like individual doctors—was operating as a cottage industry. Each entity tackled certain aspects of health care in isolation from the others. A focus on the total end-to-end experience of the consumer, in this case the patient, was conspicuously missing. The industry was data poor: medical records were kept on paper in separate physical locations, so while patients passed from one care entity to another, information about them did not. That made it impossible to identify opportunities for improvement based on data from various parts of the health-care chain. Health-care costs were steadily rising, a huge problem. People inside and outside of the industry, including members of Congress, began talking about health-care rationing, distasteful as it was, as perhaps the only viable end game for care delivery.

That was the situation in 2002, the year George Halvorson became CEO of Kaiser Permanente, the California-based health insurance company that also ran clinics and community hospitals. He saw things differently. While many of his industry peers seemed resigned to a future of rationing and hoped mainly to postpone it, he saw an option. Why not reengineer health care—that is, use information technology to integrate the information and use it to find ways to improve the cost and quality of outcomes for care delivery? Despite the fact that US health care was and is in seemingly permanent flux, Halvorson went on the offense. In so doing he created clarity for his own company and, by sharing his thinking and helping shape government policy, for many other players as well.

Rationing didn't make sense to him, first because it conjured up a dour future that didn't match the idealistic mission of health-care providers, and second because he had seen the benefits of linking clinics and hospitals in his former post as head of Health Partners, a $2 billion health plan and delivery system in Minnesota. "Rationing would be a lousy world to be in, for our business and for our patients," Halvorson explains. "I knew there were better answers, because I had had the good fortune of running a model where we owned clinics and hospitals, and we could track things using information that crossed those organizational boundaries. For example, we could focus on our patients with diabetes and co-morbidities and significantly reduce the rate of kidney failure for our patients with proactive team care that is hard to do with paper data systems."

Thanks to Halvorson's experience in Minnesota and a book he had written that captured his thinking about health care, the board of KP knew what to expect when they hired him. Halvorson had a distinct point of view: better data and its right use meant better care. He also believed that tracking care outcomes and processes could create safer care. He had seen, for instance, that it was not uncommon for patients to contract infections while in the hospital, including deadly sepsis, despite the fact that doctors and nurses were highly ethical, caring, and competent. With little data in most care sites to track the sepsis problem and get to its roots, it persisted as the number one cause of deaths in US hospitals. Also, individual hospitals focused only on what happened within their walls and had no incentive to think about the entire continuum of care for any patient. A hospital that gets a fee every time a child with asthma is admitted, for example, focuses on improving care for the time when those children are under its roof. It has no reason to seek information about what happened beforehand, including what circumstances might have triggered the asthma attack and what might have prevented it.

At the time Halvorson joined KP, it was, like Health Partners, "integrated," meaning it had businesses in many parts of the health-care chain. But to say the parts were fully connected would be misleading. There were many work sites and care departments at KP. In fact, KP had more than forty unions, eight basic medical groups, and myriad layers of caregiving and care sites. Each geographic area had its own brand and advertising campaign, and each new hospital and major care center got the latest, greatest accounting system when the facility was built—with over 125 accounting systems in total. When headquarters wanted basic month end financial information, it took a month and a half to get it. Care was "pretty good," although not good enough in Halvorson's estimation, but costs needed improvement, service levels were inconsistent, and in some cases the public image was not good, in part because the company was sometimes willing to go to court to fight over things that made patients uncomfortable.

Halvorson was a catalyst who conceived a path for KP that broke with conventional practice, based on integrating all of the pieces, not merely assembling them. "I could see that the world was going to change, and I didn't want to wait and see how those changes would affect us," Halvorson explained. "We needed team care. We needed patient-based care. I figured if we can get there first, we win, and of course our patients do too."

Halvorson was ready to go on the offense, but getting the organization to buy in was not automatic. KP employees were no different from everyone else in health care: uncertain and anxious about the future. Some wondered where health care was going and whether it would bypass KP. Was KP part of the future or stuck in the past? Other organizations that sold what they portrayed to be similar products were competing fiercely to try to knock KP out of the ring. Managers at the head of various organizational units kept their heads down, focusing on internal operations more than external issues and the future. Halvorson saw an interconnection between the ongoing beliefs and behaviors at KP and the goal of improving health care this way: improving health care depended on data; data depended on trust; trust had to be built through transparency. He set out to create both an information system and a culture that would accomplish the end goal.

Having visited with employees, major buyers, purchasers, and other constituents even before his official start date, Halvorson hit the ground running when he became CEO in 2002. Very early in his tenure he visited the KP site in Hawaii, which had just put in place a prototype of a home-grown electronic medical record information system. The system had been built by some smart people, and it had consumed a lot of money. But after two days of working with it, Halvorson concluded that it fell significantly short of the capabilities KP needed. "It couldn't do several of the key things it needed to do," Halvorson says. "I knew that if we rolled it out as it was designed, it could have caused significant damage and delayed our progress for years." Yet the idea of pulling the plug on the existing system, which had already cost KP $400 million to date, was daunting, and doing so would leave a gaping hole.

On his return to the mainland, the CEO convened a task force of seventy people, almost all doctors, to fill the gap. He asked them to identify everything they wanted a system to do and to look at every system in the world. There were no front runners. "Hire the best consultants from the best firms in the world if you have to," he told them. "Money is no object. We need to find the best option that meets our needs." That approach accomplished two things: first, it sorted through the various systems builders, pointing to two finalists and ultimately to their partner of choice, EPIC Systems of Madison, Wisconsin; second, it garnered a lot of internal support. A side benefit was the personal learning that all of the internal evaluation team members acquired from having compared so many systems.

The one potential stumbling block was the price tag for their chosen system and for the total system rebuilding and interconnectivity project: $4 billion, the biggest investment in an information system anyone at any company in the world had ever made. The KP board was accustomed to approving "big" expenditures of, say, $200 million to $400 million, but this was a different animal. Halvorson did not soft pedal. "I told them that we were betting the farm on this. I walked them through the logic, so they could see that if we didn't do it, we would have a very challenged future. If we did it but did it poorly, we would also fail. But if we computerized everything related to care delivery and did that well, it would put us ahead of the curve and keep us there for a very long time. The tool could have infinite capabilities. I told the board that once we had the system, it would be like having the Internet—we would keep finding uses we didn't know were possible."

The high stakes were not lost on the board. One recently recruited director heard Halvorson's "bet the farm" speech at his first ever board meeting. "I went home and had a sleepless night," he later told Halvorson. Nonetheless, the board approved the investment, and KP forged ahead on its new path to become a completely computerized and paperless care system—with all data on all patients instantly accessible to all caregivers.

Implementing the system was of course a huge undertaking that depended on having the right leadership. Halvorson chose Louise Liang, who had held various leadership positions in the health-care field and was also knowledgeable about quality improvement. She was meticulous, collaborative, highly organized, hands on, and fast—able to lay the tracks right in front of the train, as Halvorson put it. And importantly, she was a physician, not just a technologist, so she was respected by doctors and sensitive to the issues around quality care. Her direct line to Halvorson and authority over the existing IT department gave her the clout she needed to clear any organizational or financial blockages. With lots of effort and disciplined oversight, the system got built on time and on budget.

Meanwhile, the drive for continuous improvement and the push for combining data were showing good results as KP targeted one problem after another. Very few healthcare organizations commit to continuous improvement approaches that blend data expertise and process engineering skills with care delivery skills. Halvorson did, strongly supporting a continuous improvement model for care delivery. As one example, in 2008 the care team set a goal of reducing the death rate from sepsis from 25 to 20 percent of patients with the infection by the following year.

It took a number of months to get the right elements in place: to create the right internal data flow, to work on the culture issues in each care site so that people would get comfortable with making their information transparent from one hospital to another, and to create a common measurement and sharing process. Some people doubted it could happen, but others said, if we can do this next year, why not now? Once the pieces needed to do continuous improvement were in place, it was full steam ahead. The hospitals began to compare their numbers with each other and to pay more attention to how—and when—sepsis was treated. What was different about those with lower rates? Insights from the process improvement exercise included significantly shortening the wait for lab results and the time it took to get prescriptions filled. Speedier treatment was the best way to reduce death from that infection. With data in hand, people began to make multiple, seemingly small changes in their labs and hospital pharmacies to create that speed. The results were striking: the death rate across KP hospitals dropped from 25 percent to the targeted 20 percent—and then kept falling. It was 10 percent two years later, and by 2013 it was under 10 percent, possibly the lowest in the country.

Data opened new lines of discovery, with equally impressive results in the treatment of HIV, congestive heart failure, asthma, and stroke victims. The HIV death rate dropped to half of the national average. The new, comprehensive data flow also allowed important discoveries about stroke patients who died. Researchers found that patients who were given a statin drug in the hospital after having a stroke had a lower death rate than those who were not (6 percent versus 11 percent). No one had thought of statins as a life-changing treatment for strokes, but electronic data available to KP from millions of patients showed that they made a major difference.

KP made the conscious decision to share its findings and methods with other players in the health-care field. While it had been producing something like three hundred research reports in official medical publications a year, now it kicked into high gear, publishing nearly fifteen hundred in 2013. "We wanted to live in a world where we competed on the basis of making care better, so we decided to bring everyone else along," Halvorson says. "So, for example, we made our HIV protocols public, and we gave them away free so everyone in health care across the country would have them and could use them."

The good results from data access and process improvement boosted KP's reputation. Once the new system was in place and fully functioning, KP was rated the number one plan by JD Power, Consumer Reports, and Medicare. But the successes had import far beyond KP. They demonstrated that improving the delivery and effectiveness of health care was a better alternative than rationing. That knowledge helped to shape the health-care agenda in Washington. Halvorson even got involved in helping shape the Affordable Care Act (ACA), saying "We'd rather help structure the actions Washington takes in a positive direction rather than just reacting to what they do. We deliver care for a living, so we have a lot to offer about how care can be improved. That is good information to share with the people who regulate care. Our influence level about what to do is high when what we do clearly succeeds."

Since passage of the ACA—some would say largely because of the ACA—the market structures and competitive dynamics of the health- care industry have remained in flux as various players have tried to decide where and how to compete. Halvorson didn't soften his stance: "We are building systems-supported care, data-supported care, and science-based care in an integrated way. If we had not taken the gamble to invest in these systems and put them in place, we would look like everyone else—and the future would force itself on us. You can't always predict the world ahead, but sometimes you can create the world ahead. So we've been creating it." Pure offense.

———

HALVORSON SAW UNCERTAINTY as a call for leadership of not only his company but also the health-care industry. He found opportunity in it. He formed a specific, concrete view of what health-care delivery could be and had the courage to set the path for his company, communicating it with clarity to those whose participation he needed. That included people in government. While carving a path in uncertainty can seem like a lonely task, it ultimately involves many people. The following chapters explain how to prepare the organization to take advantage of uncertainty, transition to a new path, and make ongoing adjustments to the changing world. I start by describing a powerful managerial tool that can make *any* organization more agile.

CHECKLIST FOR PART III

✓ Are you conscious of the shortening shelf life of your core competencies, competitive advantage, and the definition of your core business? Do you ask at least four times a year: What new developments can I take advantage of to create a new need or give the customer or consumer a more compelling experience?

✓ How well do you understand the end-to-end consumer experience? Have you mapped the touch points? Do you observe consumers firsthand? Do you exercise your imagination to think of new trajectories based on your observations and insights?

✓ Have you educated yourself about new digital technologies and the use of algorithms? Is your team learning about them? Are you paying attention to digital players coming into your space? Do you regularly consider and discuss how you might use digital technology to transform your business? Do you regularly talk to people with such expertise?

✓ Are you on the lookout for new opportunities for profitable growth?

✓ How conscious are you of the human tendency to revert to what is comfortable and known? How aware are you of your psychological blockages and fears that prevent you from seeing new opportunities? Do you try to overcome your own psychological discomfort with venturing into new areas? Are you willing to make moves that are well thought out but not immediately popular?

✓ Are you willing to move with speed even if some variables are still uncertain?

PART IV

MAKING THE ORGANIZATION AGILE

CHAPTER 12

The Joint Practice Session: Transparency and Coordination

LET'S IMAGINE THAT I have been meeting with you and your colleagues for a couple of hours, and we have been discussing some of my ideas for honing your skills in sensing bends in the road ahead of others and being on the attack to create a new future. Everyone has been nodding their heads in agreement. Of course I hope that they are not just being polite. But I sense an uneasiness in the room, and it surfaces when your colleague Mary speaks up and starts to articulate the reason for it.

"Ram," she says, "this is all well and good, but we've got targets to meet under really tough conditions, and we're locked into quarterly and annual budget commitments that are non-negotiable. Wall Street, the board, and the media will slam our CEO if he doesn't deliver the numbers, and all of our commitments feed into that. The only time we could justify changing things is if we had a crisis in production or a loss of a major customer or were let down by a major supplier. So we're too busy to watch for bends in the road or speculate about what we could do to change the game."

As Mary ticks off her litany of issues, it's my turn to nod in agreement. I have heard these things before, far too often. There's the budgeting process. The numbers are frozen at the beginning of the fiscal year, as if the reality that unfolds between January 1 and December 31 is fixed. At this company, like most others, decisions about who gets more resources and who gets less are made once a year, so rigidity for that time period is built in. So, too, are quarterly and annual goals. The result is that there's no way to make changes when major uncertainty hits. Almost all companies seem to have such rigidities.

"Even if the resources were available, the incentives are all wrong," Mary continued. "Say that Matt here sees a bend in the road just ahead and figures out a great strategy to deal with it. Executing it will cut into his numbers for the year, and there go his targets, his bonus, and any chance of being promoted." She turns to Matt. "Is that a risk you'd want to take?" Matt's reply is almost instant: "Not really." Mary turns back to me. "So what can we do? We might be flexible as individuals, but how can we move on opportunities we see when the organization itself makes us rigid—and for that matter, what does it mean for an organization to be agile and flexible?"

Mary put her finger on a tough issue: it's one thing to know that the external landscape is an ever-shifting mosaic, and quite another for leaders to connect their everyday activities to those changes. Yet doing so is the only way to ensure that the organization stays relevant and preferably on the offense. Leaders have no choice but to *steer* their organization to adjust in real time and take control of uncertainty.

What makes an organization "steerable," or agile enough to be redirected quickly, is streamlining its linkage with the speed and character of the external environment.[11] That means breaking the core rigidities that commonly constrain organizations: long, drawn-out processes for making decisions through multiple layers; the slow, filtered, often sequential processing of information on its way to the decision makers; unresolved disagreements stemming from narrow perspectives and self-interest of siloed leaders; budgets and KPIs and the incentives that are tied to them, all of which are essentially fixed for a year or more at a time; and people assignments that don't get changed.

Looking forward to offering Mary some hope, I proposed a tool that can break these rigidities and allow the organization to adapt: the JPS. Developed by Sam Walton in the early years of Wal-Mart, rigorously implemented by Steve Jobs, and used by Alan Mulally in the masterful turnaround at Ford, the JPS is the most powerful mechanism I have ever seen for integrating and steering the organization.

Mary was skeptical. "Ram, are you talking about another *meeting?*" she asked. "We have them in spades!" "Yes," I replied, "they do require that people come together face to face, but they are unlike other meetings in crucial ways. People practice working as a team to identify opportunities and solve problems, and they make adjustments to their individual priorities, resources, and other things like budgets and KPIs. Once they get the rhythm of this mechanism, they like it, they want it, and they find it energizing." I then explained those crucial differences.

Not Just Another Meeting

Weekly staff meetings and monthly review meetings have been the bane of collaboration. They are often boring, time wasting, and energy draining. They even generate fear. Consider a typical business review, in which the focus is on last period's results. It's not uncommon for the boss, in a show of power, to single out those who missed their targets and grill them. There's little coaching, and few people learn anything. Leaders are not concerned about the impact on people's morale, focus, or ability to work together. The result: people go into those meetings feeling anxious and defensive and leave embarrassed and drained of energy.

Joint practice sessions have the opposite effect. They are based on the premise that when information is transparent to everyone in the group at the same time, people can form a common view of the total picture. They are more willing and better equipped to make trade-offs and adjustments spontaneously. Decisions are made, bottlenecks get broken, people are energized, and the organization gets results. It's a proven and highly successful way to knit the group together and steer it onto a new path.

I'll illustrate how a JPS works by describing examples in three different industries. Mulally used the JPS to turn around Ford's top team. "Jenn Hedley," CEO of a business unit of a large financial services company, used similar practice sessions after the financial crisis to extend the company's lead by taking advantage of digital technology and consumers' changed behavior. Jay Galeota, as president of Merck's Hospital & Specialty Care business (he's now Merck's chief strategy and business development officer and president of emerging businesses), used the JPS to steer his organization onto a different track when competitive uncertainties went against it. Before going into these examples, though, let me sum up the principles you will see unfolding as we proceed:

- The JPS includes all the critical people whose work is highly interdependent, meaning that their goals, priorities, information, and outputs affect and are affected by each other's. Additional people are invited to attend when their viewpoints or expertise are needed, but the greatest benefit is achieved when the core group meets together frequently; once a week is common. The most important group for steering an organization includes the CEO and her direct reports. Attendance is mandatory, at least initially, so all members can practice together.

- Transparency rules. All members put forward their progress on their five to ten most critical tasks—the good, the bad, and the ugly. Dashboards clearly show which tasks are on target (coded green), which ones are encountering difficulty (yellow), and which are stalled (red). This creates a shared picture of the current realities so that everyone can see what the issues are. Information presented openly and with ruthless honesty is central to steering the organization and getting it to move quickly. Candor becomes a habit, because people who haven't been forthcoming are invariably exposed; they will have to either change their behavior or drop out.

- The group members focus on getting to the root cause of every task that is off track and helping the person work through it. This, of course, is the exact opposite of traditional meetings that put people on the defensive. Yet it takes only a few rounds of practice for team members to spontaneously offer help—which is the first indication that the rigidity of silos is being broken and the organization is becoming agile.

- Transparency allows people to see how decisions affect each part of the business and the common goals. If one person's target is lowered, someone else's must increase so that the team as a whole can still achieve the overall target; if one person's priorities change, resources may have to shift. Those trade-offs and adjustments can be made on the spot, and everyone understands the reasons for them. An uptick in the economy might create the opportunity to sell more premium products, for example, but additional funds to launch and market them may have to be extracted from another part of the business. The transparency allows facts, not politics, to rule, so individuals are willing to spontaneously volunteer their resources and people to achieve the goals and priorities the group deems most important. Conflicts become visible and are resolved.

- Observations about what is happening in the external context and how it is affecting the business are built into the discussions. Members present their own perspectives but converge on a common view, which stimulates their sense of urgency to behave differently.

- Team members can better steer their parts of the organization because they can visualize the progress of the total group and know what the hurdles are on a weekly basis.

The frequency of the JPS conditions people's behavior and attitudes. Think about how a winning basketball team stays synchronized as the game moves: the players develop the ability through practice on the court. It's no different for an executive team. Through repetition, collaborative behavior becomes routine, and the behaviors tend to spill into other parts of the company. Decisions and adjustments are made faster not just within the JPS, and the organization moves with speed. Those who are loners or withhold information usually succumb to peer pressure or leave.

The ability to adjust better and faster to current realities obviously increases your advantage over other companies. What's not so obvious is that joint practice broadens the thinking of functional leaders and prepares them for potential roles as P&L leaders, general managers, or CEOs.

The JPS may seem to consume a lot of high-powered leaders' time, but it actually frees them up by eliminating the need for preplanning meetings and the tedious preparation of those PowerPoint slides you hope will save you when the grilling begins. It is also psychologically liberating. More subtle, but profoundly important, is that the competitive tendency to hoard information is trumped by the clear collaborative benefits of transparency and sharing. Time and again I have observed that once the rhythm of the JPS takes hold, usually after about six rounds, people become more selfless as they see the results of working together to achieve the team's targets. The organization becomes still more responsive as the next layer begins to do the same.

Sam Walton's JPS

Sam Walton made the JPS his central steering mechanism. Key people gathered together—store managers, logistical people, advertising people, and buyers—and worked as a team to ensure that Wal-Mart delivered on its mission of providing the lowest prices. (In the early days they met daily; as the organization grew, the frequency shifted to weekly.) They focused on a handful of questions: What are customers asking for that we don't have? Is there too much in the store that is not selling? How does our price for a given product compare with our competitors'? (Participants gathered this information by walking the competitors' aisles.) And notably, how many customers come into a store and buy nothing? Having been in retail myself for many years working in my family's shoe shop in India, I found this question very insightful. It perhaps helps explain why Wal-Mart was so successful.

Those sessions, in which all the key people were playing on the court, made Wal-Mart agile, able to respond promptly to customers' changing needs. By building the rhythm of daily practice they could resolve conflicts quickly and make decisions on the spot. If, for example, the stores were running short of sweaters, a buyer would volunteer to get them within four working days. Everyone in the room got the same sharp picture of customers' and competitive behavior. Their mind-set became outside-in. By seeing the whole business, each person grew along with Walton to be a broader thinker. Although individual accountability was not lost, collaboration became part of their DNA. Business results followed: able to get the right merchandise into the store quickly, Wal-Mart had the highest inventory turns and sales per square foot at the time.

Steve Jobs set up a similar mechanism when he returned as CEO of Apple in 1997. He had learned it during his sojourn at Pixar. Jobs greatly admired Pixar CEO Ed Catmull, whose daily practice was to have every person who was developing sketches for an animated film post them online at the end of each day. The following morning Catmull and John Lasseter, the chief creative officer, would review the work and encourage other artists to critique it. I contend that this intense process underlies Pixar's fourteen consecutive box office successes—the equivalent of winning consecutive Olympic gold medals.

Jobs instituted a four-hour Monday morning session at Apple at which people whose interdependence was crucial discussed one or more products. At times the group included suppliers flown in from Taiwan and China. Jobs wanted everyone in the room listening to each piece of information simultaneously, believing that the resulting dialogue and debate would foster better integration. And indeed, this practice got experts with sizable egos to support decisions that were best for the product they were developing, not just for their own silos.

A JPS in Financial Services

When Jenn Hedley joined "Long & Short Investment Group" as CEO of its Wealth Management business in 2009, customers were still feeling the aftershocks of the global financial meltdown and placing a new premium on the trustworthiness of a financial services firm. Long & Short had a strong brand, with a reputation for good service, and hadn't experienced the problems that so many in the financial services industry had. Hedley and her team saw an opportunity to capture new business. But to fully succeed, the organization needed speed, and that meant streamlining the connection between the people running Wealth Management at headquarters and those in the field who interface with clients. They understood that an end-to-end customer experience starts before a customer's first transaction (with advertising, for example) and ends only after the customer leaves the firm. In financial services, that can be a long time; the relationship can last for the customer's lifetime—and beyond, through the next generation. They also knew that the best customer experiences are integrated, meaning that all the internal working parts of the organization are synchronized in a way that is invisible to the consumer.

Hedley and her team systematically examined the components of the customer experience and looked for enhancements that would make it best in class. They knew they could tap into Long & Short's strong cultural DNA, whereby associates took great pride in doing right by customers. They also recognized that a great customer experience depended on having a best-in-class associate experience—that is, on the satisfaction of the associates who directly served customers. Their attitude had an enormous influence on customer satisfaction, and in turn, the long-term relationships that developed with satisfied customers energized the associates.

Hedley was new to the organization, so she needed a deep but quick education in the experiences of these customers, their emerging needs as the world changed around them, possible improvements that could help both customers and the associates, and where Long & Short could leverage its success by creating new opportunities. She traveled exten-sively to all parts of the country, getting input firsthand by meeting with customers and frontline associates. During an early visit, the leader of a site that handles customer calls gave her a special gift: an iPod loaded with twenty hours of recorded customer calls. She listened to every minute (and continues the habit to this day, listening to twenty hours of calls each month) in order to get a pulse on how clients felt about their experiences and listening for subtle clues about how to improve them. In every conversation she pushed people to say what was really on their minds. "Speed mat-ters a lot," she explained, "and part of speed is getting can-did feedback quickly. There's a natural tendency for people to be polite, but we had to pierce through that so we didn't waste time trying to figure out what they were really saying. We wanted their ideas unfiltered, even if it hit us right be-tween the eyes."

Hedley also wanted to bridge any gaps in understanding between the field and the home office on issues the team needed to jointly address. She organized summits at which groups of people from the field were brought to the home office to voice their concerns while the top team basically sat back and listened for two days. She encouraged candor by going off script and asking direct questions, because, she says, "When you ask a direct question, it's pretty easy to tell whether the person is giving an honest answer or just being political." In one instance, when Hedley sensed that a field manager was holding back, she asked him what was both-ering him. He looked around, wondering if he was really supposed to give an honest answer, but thought to himself, "I really do want to improve the place, so I'll take a chance." He described a problem he was having with how the branch office interfaced with the regional sites, and while it was a prickly organizational issue, it rang true with the senior team. Before each summit concluded, the senior team reviewed with the summit participants all the issues that were raised and made decisions about how to prioritize and address them.

To broaden the lens beyond Long & Short, Hedley sent people from the branches, regional sites, and headquarters to various places known for their world-class customer experience—places like Disneyworld and the Ritz Carlton in the United States, but also to a diverse range of companies in Europe and Asia. And to keep the information flowing between the field and the senior team, she brought people from the branches to the home office on temporary assignments for six months at a time. An internal social networking site was created to get unfiltered feedback from the front lines. A program called "Voice of the Customer Ambassadors" was formed, in which people across the country were charged with collecting feedback about problem areas and making suggestions for addressing them.

By summer of 2009 the team had established a total of forty-five work streams, each related to a specific aspect of the customer or associate experience. Some of these streams related to new opportunities and offerings. Others related to "rocks" that needed to be removed from the path to smooth out some aspect of the customer or associate experience. A number involved multiple organizational silos at which an end-to-end review needed to be completed.

Because of the interdependencies across the organization, the depth of the likely changes, and the need for speed, these work streams had to be managed differently from the traditional processes. "As we proceeded to address the opportunities we identified, we needed very regular updates on what was working, what wasn't working out quite as planned, and we needed to make corrections along the way," Hedley explains. "We needed to get the real story about what was happening, so we could take action then and there and move on. We had to meet frequently enough to make the midcourse corrections, use the new information that was coming in, and drive that into decision making. The cadence, specificity, and discipline around that structure would make all the difference in terms of ongoing communication, buy in, and the speed with which we could operate. It was also very important culturally to demonstrate senior management's commitment to change and our focus on the details."

Hedley initiated a weekly JPS (though she didn't use that term) of her direct reports every Friday afternoon. In these sessions the group made decisions and trade-offs about resources and people, changed some operating priorities, and developed a full picture of progress and what was getting in the way. The weekly frequency instilled a sense of urgency in each member of the team. Her choice of day and time was purposeful. "I told them I'd stay as long as we needed to, whether it was two hours or five hours or all night long, knowing full well that people would be anxious to start their weekends.

"My point was to have the meetings often enough that folks didn't have time to build a huge PowerPoint deck each time, and instead they'd bring their real thoughts. The short joint session time would also create a fast pace, to make us more decisive and move to action sooner."

As people became used to the meetings, they got right to the point and jumped quickly to the actions that needed to be taken. They found they didn't need to spend a lot of time preparing for meetings and scrapped the PowerPoint slides and rehearsals, freeing up time to drive projects to completion. People who reported to the participants were freed up as well.

In 2010, as change was taking hold and progress was being made, Hedley and her team turned to other important opportunities. Technology was having a profound impact in the marketplace, as a product and also as a means of changing the total customer experience. The first iPad was released that year, and companies like Amazon, Netflix, Google, and Facebook were interacting with consumers in entirely new ways. Long & Short had a strong legacy of being an innovative leader, including in technology. Why couldn't they harness the power of things like digital capabilities, big data, and analytics to take the customer experience to a whole new level?

Hedley started hiring experts in areas such as data analytics, information technology architecture, algorithms, and the science of segmentation. The senior team worked with these experts to identify ten technology-related activities that had the potential to make a big impact on customers—things like using big data to resegment the market, enhancing Long & Short's Web presence, leveraging data and analytics for a more personalized customer experience, creating various mobile applications, and updating the company's telephone contact center. Each of these projects had its own business case, its own resource needs, its own time frame, and its own person directly responsible for making decisions and accountable for getting the job done.

But while everyone who worked on these projects understood what each other's projects were supposed to accomplish, they were often siloed. The people working on those activities had to see how they related to the others. The joint practice meetings Hedley had established in 2009 were expanded to help the team see how those projects connected and how each silo's work had to be adapted and could leverage off the others to transform the customer experience. "We had to get both buy-in and understanding of how the pieces of the strategy were going to be integrated. And we had to road test them, so we wanted the chief marketing officer, the chief digital officer, the head of distribution, the CFO, and so on all talking about it simultaneously to make sure all aspects were being considered." The JPSs helped the team design an integrated system in which highly advanced technologies and algorithms to facilitate customer interactions worked well together and provided a smooth experience for the customer.

Those sessions continue. By coming together weekly, the team have become steadily better at using real-time feedback for continuous change. They have increased the organization's agility and steerability. Hedley says of the JPS: "Our governance mechanism survives and thrives. The group changes based on what we're working on, but we need it at every stage to continuously adapt to real time feedback and reinforce and monitor change."

Steering Ford to Survival

When Alan Mulally joined Ford in 2006 after spending his entire career at Boeing, he faced the ultimate uncertainty: whether Ford would survive. Ford's market share was sinking as Japanese competitors gained share and generated cash in the US market, while Ford was hemorrhaging cash. Pressure also came from the real possibility that GM and

Chrysler might go into bankruptcy, which would wipe out their debt and free them to price more aggressively, while Ford's enormous debt remained on its balance sheet. Bill Ford, the CEO and executive chairman, had told his board of directors that the company needed a new CEO and that he would, if necessary, be willing to step down even from the chair position. If the company went into bankruptcy the family would lose control.

In his very first week Mulally introduced a weekly JPS to take place every Thursday; his name for it was business plan review (BPR). All senior leaders were required to attend. This was a shock to these people, who were used to working autonomously with an entirely different rhythm. They were accustomed to "meetings week," five days each month spent in nonstop gatherings,[12] classically ineffective and short on candor and accountability. The BPRs were held every Thursday without fail, and Mulally used them to condition the top team to become change agents. He made the rules perfectly clear: reports on progress toward the company's turnaround goals were to be succinct and honest, and facts—not politics or personality—ruled the day. "Clear working-together principles, practices, and expected behaviors are basics of my management system," Mulally says. Attendance was mandatory. I was told by a member of that team that one executive who worked outside of the United States asked Mulally whether he had to attend. Mulally told him that he had a choice, either be there or. . . . He didn't have to finish the sentence.

Mulally used those BPRs to sharpen his team's perceptual acuity. "We talk about the worldwide business environment at that moment—things like the economy, the energy and technology sectors, global labor, government relations, demographic trends, what our competitors are doing, what

is going on with our customers," he told a McKinsey inter-
viewer. "Of course, we are all out there all the time as part
of our jobs, going around the world. The BPR process is the
foundation. It provides a fantastic window on the world—
the whole team knows everything that is going on. Then we
take it a step further and discuss how those trends are likely
to evolve. Looking ahead is critical. We talk about more than
what our customers value right now. We talk about the forces
in the world that are going to shape what they will value in
the future."[13]

Those same meetings were crucial in relentlessly driving
accountability and execution of the steps Ford was taking to
put itself on the new path of Mulally's comprehensive five-
year strategy and plan. Each BPR incorporated repetition of
the common goal and disciplined revisiting of operational
targets, which were displayed in charts color-coded red, yellow, or green and placed on the walls along with photos of
the leadership team member responsible for the results.[14]
This room became the equivalent of a team's basketball
court. Week after week, progress since the previous meeting—or lack thereof—was on the charts for all to see. Bottlenecks were exposed, and Mulally addressed them on the
spot. The impact of any changes in one silo were simultaneously visible to every other silo. This was a new way of sharing information in a world where leaders were accustomed
to managing the information flow for self-preservation, but
as they adapted to it, they came to value it.

Mulally reinforced the importance of teamwork through
his demand for mutual respect and collaborative problem
solving in the meetings and took it on himself to ensure that
everyone was behaving like a team player. "The accountability and the responsibility here is to help everybody on

the team turn reds into yellow and greens, and to deliver increasing earnings and increasing cash flow every year," Mulally explained.[15] When Mark Fields, head of the Americas at Ford, mustered the courage to admit problems with the launch of the Edge crossover vehicle at an early BPR, Mulally applauded his candor, then calmly turned to the team and asked, "Who can help Mark with this?" The response was gratifying: people volunteered suggestions, resources, and ways to change priorities to help.[16] The entire top team from the old Ford remained as Mulally transitioned the company, apart from some members who retired, one who left for a better job, and another who was released. Yet the mind-set shifted, decisions were made faster, and actions were coordinated. People took great satisfaction in their meaningful accomplishments. What's more, it became clear that the JPSs broadened functional leaders into business-as-a-whole leaders and tested their readiness for bigger jobs as presidents of P&L centers, country managers, and more. Case in point: Mark Fields is now Ford's CEO.

THERE IS AS YET no better way to make an organization agile than the JPS. It is a necessary tool in times of structural uncertainty. I have now seen the adoption of the JPS by several companies. The next chapter describes how Keurig Green Mountain got theirs started.

CHAPTER 13

How Keurig Green Mountain Adopted the Joint Practice Session

KEURIG GREEN MOUNTAIN made headlines in May 2014 when Coca-Cola increased its stake in the coffee roaster cum beverage technology company from 10 to 16 percent. Coke does not make passive investments in other companies, so the move sparked a lot of speculation about what the alliance might mean, especially for big players such as Dunkin Donuts and Starbucks, which had been bearing down on Green Mountain's personalized coffee brewers market. Meanwhile another important event was taking place behind the scenes in a conference room where CEO Brian Kelley was establishing a mechanism to make the organization easy to steer onto a new path that would put it on the offense.

Green Mountain began its life in the early 1980s as a tiny coffee roaster in Waterbury, Vermont, then expanded and went public in the early 1990s. Its purchase of Keurig, the manufacturer of single-serve coffeemakers, in 2006 laid the foundation for supercharged growth. After Kelley surprised the beverage industry by leaving a high-level job at Coke to become Green Mountain's CEO in 2012, he led an aggressive push to accelerate innovation in the brewing machines and the beverage portion packs. To broaden the Keurig system's appeal to consumers, he formed partnerships with many coffee and tea brands to provide "K cups" for Keurig's machines. Revenues and earnings per share kept growing by double-digit percentages for several years, reaching $4.3 billion and $3.39 billion, respectively, by 2013. Market capitalization jumped from $4 bilion to $24 billion in just two years.

As Kelley saw it, those achievements from the company's small beginnings were fuel to get the company onto the next new platform for growth. But Kelley was as focused on steering the organization as he was on strategy. He knew he had to shift attention and resources to execute. After all, there were plenty of other players in the consumer beverage space, and some had introduced home brewers of their own. In January 2014 Kelley launched what he later came to call JPSs to integrate all the functions across the business, involving some twenty-five top people.

He had asked me to help design and facilitate the inaugural meeting. With just a brief introduction, I took them through an exercise on the spot. I asked the members to write down their top three priorities for the upcoming quarter. Accustomed to planning sessions that focused one, two, or three years out, they were surprised by the short time frame, but my intention was to help them focus on executing the short-term steps that were part of their journey. They took several minutes, and then I asked them to list these priorities across the bottom of a blank piece of paper, and above each, to draw bars, smokestack style, for the five critical tasks associated with that priority. We went around the room so each person could explain his or hers. It was the first time they had heard each other's priorities and tasks in detail. Then came the fun part—I asked them to grab the markers strewn on the tables to color-code those critical tasks red, yellow, or green for how they were progressing as of that day.

We gathered the twenty-five sheets of paper and taped them to the walls, and we all stood in a semicircle and looked. "What do you see?" I asked. People were noticeably uncomfortable that there was lots of red and very little green. "This is normal for any company," I reassured them. "Keep looking." As they did, team members started to notice that a number of the reds had something in common: the people with critical technical expertise that they depended on were stretched too thin. We discussed why those people were overburdened, and it came to light that the hiring of more such experts had been approved and budgeted for, but those jobs had not been filled for a long time. The CEO turned to the people from HR and asked what was getting in the way. It turned out that the senior HR leaders and operating leaders had not been making themselves available for interviews. The solution to this bottleneck was obvious.

Other issues also surfaced. Two leaders were driving similar critical tasks. Should those be combined? Was one more important than the other? A decision was made on the spot to combine two tasks into one. Another critical task was red because a supplier had been lagging behind, and again people put their heads together to figure out how to overcome the problem in the short run. No one had to say that the purpose of the mechanism was to help individuals get over the hump, to go from red and yellow to green. It was simply happening.

The group reconvened six times over the next three months. When Kelley saw people between the meetings, he solicited feedback on how they thought the new JPS mechanism was working. One comment he occasionally heard from some of his direct reports was that while the sessions helped expose some problems and moved some things along, it felt like he was using them for control and imposing a layer of bureaucracy. Those comments bothered Kelley, and he pondered them as he approached the mid-April session, which I had again been asked to facilitate.

It was time to dispel the concerns and make the purpose and intended benefits of this kind of meeting more explicit and to build on the foundation that had been established. Kelley opened the JPS in April 2014 by reminding everyone of the vision they had for the company in 2020. He brought that vision to life with a credible, concrete description of the company's strategic direction, and he energized the group with a three-minute video he had prepared to remind them of the company's success to date and its unfulfilled promise. "We have to stay together on this journey," he reminded them. In particular, they had to be sure to execute on two projects that were destiny shaping for the company and even the industry, both of which involved nearly half the people in the room. "Given the timing for launch, we have to move with urgency and synchronize our work. That's what these sessions are for," Kelley said. "We'll face hiccups, whether it's failures of suppliers or new information from our trials, and we can't afford to delay decisions about reassigning people or adjusting resources as those things crop up."

Then I stepped in, as Kelley and I had agreed, to explain the joint practice concept more fully and encourage them to take the viewpoint of the broader goal versus what was in the interest of their own disciplines. I noted the value of making information available to everyone simultaneously and without filters, and of being in the same room when adjustments and decisions had to be made. I reminded them that that's exactly what had happened spontaneously at the January meeting. "It's one thing to talk about alignment," I said. "When you discover where the misalignments in priorities and goals and resources are and then do something about them—that's when the alignment actually happens."

One of the team members reacted candidly: "I've been trying to go along with this since we started these meetings in January, but I really didn't get it. Now I get it." If others weren't convinced yet, they were about to be by the discussion and outcomes that followed.

Kelley had created a template to make it easier to identify problem spots on the various priorities from week to week. Team members were to complete it for each of their top three priorities. Column 1 showed which of the ten companywide priorities was being supported. Column 2 described the critical tasks associated with that priority and identified the person who was directly responsible for that task. Column 3 stated how progress would be measured. Column 4 showed what—really who, by name—the task depended on, especially those who were beyond their immediate control. Column 5 showed the blockages or major hurdles that had to be overcome.

Kelley had previously given the template to two team members who oversaw two of the company's most important projects and asked them to complete it before the meeting. First up was Tara. Her task was highly complex and depended on resolving some tough technical issues. As she took people through the template, they asked a lot of questions, which she answered. It became clear that she needed more engineers and more input from people in other departments. The decision to transfer some people from another project was made right then and there. Someone mentioned that she should include an individual with a certain expertise, and it was agreed that his boss would free up some of his time. The discussion took an hour and a half, and in that time, Tara was assured that she would get what she needed—in this case people, not money—to avoid delays. She became more energized knowing that with those adjustments, she would be able to continue to make progress.

The group went through the second template the same way. As the discussion evolved, another need came to light, this one with a hefty price tag. It was clear that going on the offense with more innovation required a sizable commitment of money over three years. The money wouldn't come from thin air; they had to reallocate it. The group as a whole discussed where it might come from; then Charlie, whose budget was relatively big for a part of the business that was slowing, offered to cut his budget by that amount. It was a heroic act, taken from the viewpoint of the overall company. It wouldn't have been right to take money from Charlie without adjusting his key performance indicators, so that change was made soon after.

Toward the end of the meeting I proposed some questions to reflect on, one of which was: What are the two game breakers, the things that could make everything go to hell? That brought Tara back to an unresolved technical problem, and it came right out that the answer might need to come from outside the company. The group decided that they needed to assign someone full time to search the world.

So twenty-five people had spent a full day in this meeting. Was it worth it? I asked. The resounding response was yes, because they could see the total picture of the business; they had identified the blockages and in many cases had fixed them. They knew what they had to focus on when they went back to work, and that it was aligned with what was happening across the company. The JPS was new, yet it had become a routine, and a welcome one that gave the company newfound agility. It has now become a quick weekly review where each leader reports out on progress against their key priorities.

———

JOINT PRACTICE SESSIONS are a crucial steering mechanism at the top of the organization, where silos must be broken to achieve the company's deliverables and move to the new path, but they are equally useful at other organizational levels where joint decision making is required. Delegating those decisions is not enough. You have to dissect your organization's decision-making processes to ensure that the what, who, and how of decision making are in sync with the speed and nature of change. A new path will likely require big shifts in decision making. Failure to make those shifts is a source of rigidity. The next chapter explains how to use decision making as a tool for making the organization agile.

CHAPTER 14

The What, Who, and How of Decision Making: Zeroing in on the Organization's Critical Decision Nodes

LET'S ASSUME YOU have identified a new path for the business. Steering onto it almost certainly means changing the way pivotal decisions are made. Your ability to dissect your organization's decision making is an important part of how you steer it through the big bends in the road and also make small adjustments as you navigate. Chances are you will need to put different people in charge of some decisions, ensure that they are taking different information into account—importantly, the externals—and are including different kinds of expertise, such as mathematical capability, with a greater level of collaboration. Unless you drive the necessary changes in decision making, your organization could seize up and your great plans shrivel. You must identify the crucial decision nodes: the specific points in the organization at which the most critical decisions are made.[17]

Start with the *what*. What are the most critical decisions, the ones that are pivotal to the business and that drive many other decisions? These will point you to the nodes. Then consider the *who*. Who should be responsible for getting these decisions made and held accountable for them, and who else should be involved in making them? Pay attention to who is exercising power; it might not be the official decision maker. And don't leave it at that; pay attention to *how* those decisions are being made: what factors are taken into account, what information is used, how many alternatives are shaped, what is emphasized, what rules of thumb are used. Decisions increasingly require inputs from multiple vantage points and areas of expertise. Is collaboration truly happening?

Attending to the what, who, and how of decision making at the ground level will get you to the crux of what drives or stalls the process of moving in the new direction and dealing with new uncertainties. It will keep you on the attack.

Identifying Decision Nodes

To find the decision nodes that matter most, work backward from the crucial actions that must be taken. Succeeding in local markets in other countries, for example, means understanding those markets better and acting faster than local competitors, so you can go on the offense. Decisions about product mix, pricing, and the like will probably need to be

made closer to the action, which for many global companies means putting local P&L managers in charge of all the
product lines and functions for a country. That becomes an
important decision node for winning in that market.

A node can be an individual, but more often it is a group of
people, with one person ultimately responsible. In chapter
12 we looked at how Jenn Hedley of Long & Short's Wealth
Management business used the JPS to bring the various parts
of the organization together to create an integrated platform
that would put them on the offense. That group was a decision node, and she was ultimately in charge of it. Her starting place for identifying it and who should be in it was the
"action" she wanted to achieve: a technology platform that
combined sophisticated software and algorithms to give
customers a compelling end-to-end experience. The experts
who were working on various IT projects had to be involved,
as did those with deep insights into the consumer, so she
included leaders from sales and marketing. That became a
new node. The JPSs she held every week got the people in
this node—in technology and marketing and sales—working
together as never before and continually adjusting their priorities, resources, and KPIs.

Leaders facing new challenges often make changes in organizational structure or key people. Such moves might be
necessary but by themselves miss what is perhaps the most
important factor: looking with fresh eyes at decision nodes
to get the moving parts of the organization working together
in ways that are different from the past. Recently I was working with "Bill Navarro," the CEO of a portable medical equipment company, who had a very ambitious three-year plan
but was concerned that the organization wasn't moving fast
enough. I asked him what the company's success depended

on, and he replied that it needed to launch five new products the next year, five the year after that, and another five in year three. That's an ambitious goal, all the more so since this technology-based company had only launched a total of three products over the past three years. Reaching it would requires rigorous thinking about the decision nodes.

"Do you have the technical talent?" I asked.

"Not enough," he said. He explained the difficulties of finding people with the right mix of training and experience in both health care and software—not just any software, of course, but the ability to write sophisticated code for complex algorithms. Such people were extremely rare.

"What are you doing to recruit them?" the questioning continued.

"We've been neither aggressive nor successful. So now we are struggling to find a new head of HR, someone who can put some energy into solving this problem."

It struck me that such a decision could not be delayed, and it was one he himself needed to own and spend time on. He was the decision node. The product launches, however, were a different story. Their importance suggested that a crucial decision node was the one that weighed and appropriately integrated inputs about the customer, technology, regulation, manufacturing, sales, and finance. Whoever was going to be charged with making those decisions would need some special integrating skills, such as having the bandwidth to take in information from many sources, the creativity to shape different alternatives, and the courage to make a judgment call and execute on it. To keep information from being distorted, the right people had to be involved simultaneously. The decision maker needs to get the group comfortable sharing information and making trade-offs.

Bill will need to spend significant time and energy attending to both of those important decision nodes. First, he must be deeply engaged in recruiting a new HR director: he knows better than anyone what kind of talent is needed, and his personal involvement will be a magnet for attracting a high-caliber person. Second, he needs to check in frequently on the node that will make decisions about what products to develop. He needs to watch to see if the information flow and communication in that node is such that the participants get a full picture of the trade-offs that must be made. Do they resolve the issues promptly? And do they muster the resources needed to act on their decisions? If not, something has to change to break those rigidities. It's up to Bill to keep the decisions humming; if he doesn't focus on those two crucial nodes, he will not be able to bring the five new products he needs online in each of the next three years. If he does, the string of successes will place him squarely on the attack.

Charting a new path may require creating an entirely new node. Chapter 3 discussed GE's move into the Industrial Internet and its potential as a source of strong growth for GE. Transforming the company into a major player in the digital age would bring it into competition with companies skilled in software analytics and algorithms such as IBM. CEO Jeff Immelt saw that GE would need a totally new capability in these areas to service industrial customers—which would also be the foundation for ultimately transforming GE's design, manufacturing, and services capabilities. To succeed in this monumental shift, he created a new decision node that would not only create a new business but also serve as the lever to transform GE for the new age. He placed it in Silicon Valley, far away from headquarters and in the nexus of where the talent resides; recruited Bill Ruh from Cisco to head it; and funded it with several hundred million dollars, even though GE was in the midst of a major cost-cutting project in the aftermath of the financial meltdown. He had the new node reporting to Mark Little, head of corporate R&D, but he interacts directly and frequently with Ruh, a clear indication of the importance assigned to the node. It is no accident that GE is now number one in the Industrial Internet. The company's transformation is moving rapidly, and this digital capability will be the key to integrating the recent acquisition of Alstom, the French maker of heavy industrial products such as turbines and high-speed trains.

Assigning the Leaders of Critical Nodes

It's essential to have the right people in charge of your most critical decisions, but changing them is often very personal; psychological contracts can interfere with good judgment. Many times I have seen an otherwise tough-minded leader ignore the fact—obvious to others—that an individual in charge of a decision node is blocking progress. I saw this play out at "Acme Media," a large communications company that was struggling to transition from print to digital. The top team had met repeatedly to discuss the impact of digitization on their business, and no one disputed that they had to break away from print and do it fast. But every time the group convened, they were in the very same position—still waiting to take those first steps to reinvent the business— while earnings from the print business continued to slip.

Frustrated by the lack of progress and the risk the company was undertaking by not transforming its core business, "Jack," the CEO, had to pinpoint the blockage. As he thought about the situation, he came to realize that "Sarah," the person he had chosen to drive the transformation, was herself the problem. She had access to plenty of resources and had direct communication lines to all the other senior leaders, but she was not making any decisions to recruit people with digital expertise and didn't even seem curious about it. Jack had every reason to want Sarah to succeed; he had worked with her for many years and greatly respected her talents. But as he sensed that her heart just wasn't in it, the picture became clear: Sarah wasn't pushing the move from print to digital because she simply didn't want to. She had made her career in print; it was her comfort zone.

Then came the challenge of figuring out what to do, and harder yet, doing it. After a lot of inner turmoil and many sleepless nights, Jack overcame his psychological barriers. He tried to retain Sarah by giving her a long-term contract to remain head of print media, although he knew she might leave when she saw print becoming a smaller slice of the total business. And he mustered the courage to recruit a new person to spearhead digital media. With a new person in charge of the node, and new kinds of talent brought into it soon after, decisions were made, and the new business began to take hold.

I have also witnessed many similar situations in which a single individual is slowing an important transition yet goes unchallenged because he or she has power, resources, informal networks, or indispensable skills. In one case, a division president was frustrated by the indecisiveness of a direct report who had forty critical people in his unit. The president knew exactly who was slowing things down. When I asked him why he didn't do something about it, he replied, "He's the CEO's favorite." Did the CEO know that this person was a procrastinator? The president hadn't thought about that. He plotted the milestones and meticulously tracked progress against them, then mustered the confidence to put the evidence on the table.

While problems in dealing with individuals may stir up sympathies or unarticulated doubts, you can't allow the social system to get jammed. Let realism rule in gauging whether the person can change. It's been my experience that while a few simple habits can change if the person works at it, fundamental behaviors do not. Suppressing that behavior might work for a short period, but when the going gets rough, people tend to revert to their old patterns.

To free up the steering, put performance reviews aside and use common sense to answer three simple questions about the individuals you put in charge of decision nodes: Does this person have the attitude, the necessary social skills, and the right expertise?

Does this person have the attitude for it? Many people will shift gears and attack the new priorities with gusto, provided their boss takes the time to make the direction clear. Alan Mulally at Ford changed tack without cleaning house, as did Lou Gerstner at IBM in the 1990s, when he reset the direction, reducing the dependence on mainframe computers in favor of software and services, and pulled the company back from the brink of failure.

But some people won't change. If someone resists too long, you have to remedy the situation before the organization calcifies. I refer again to the rule of 98–2, which I introduced in chapter 10: 2 percent of people in a company heavily influence the remaining 98 percent. Are they flexible and agile enough to buy into the new direction? In many cases, just one or two people carry heavy weight.

Does the person have the necessary social skills? I'm not referring here to being a good cocktail party conversationalist. The skill is to ask the right questions, actively seek external information and opposing views, play umpire and coach, and get people in the node to work things through together as a team—without the need for 100 percent consensus. The person must be able to manage the relationships for a new purpose, a new direction, while keeping everyone focused on the time-based goal. He has to connect with other decision makers. And he has to demonstrate the requisite behaviors. Candor, for example, is contagious.

Does the person have the right expertise? The reality is that in many fast-changing situations a totally new set of decision makers, who possess new kinds of expertise or at least are open to including others with that expertise, may have to be brought in and be given enough power for them to be effective.

Pinpointing the Right Expertise

You must be clear and specific about who needs to be in the node. A common strategy today is to use mathematical capability to transform the customer experience. In that case, the node must include people with the expertise, along with people who understand the consumer and market competition, traditional and new.

The question then is: Where in the organization should people with these required new skills be housed? And further, to whom should they report, so that their expertise is incorporated into key decisions? If they are expert in decision technology, the instinctive answer is often to put them in the information technology area, with the analytics team leader reporting to the head of IT. But that arrangement is far from ideal. Bright as they are, people in IT departments tend to be narrowly oriented. It is better to have the people with important new math capabilities be part of the nodes that tackle broader decisions. They should work directly with line people and/or the CEO or president to influence the company strategy and help find new sources of revenue and ways to increase customer satisfaction. For example, to ensure that algorithmic thinking is incorporated in decisions that affect the entire business, Nike recently decided that the head of predictive analytics would report directly to the president of the company, not the head of IT.

In another instance, the leaders of a medical equipment company developed a strategy to produce "Gizmo 2020," a portable device that would send and receive digitized medical images. They realized that while the engineering team had the medical and scientific expertise to produce the device, few of them knew enough about the mathematics underlying the sensors, data analytics, and algorithms required. These traditional product designers would look at incorporating algorithms into Gizmo 2020 from an incremental perspective, whereas those skilled in analytics would reconceptualize the device. They would have algorithms at the center of the design and allow other product features to be customized around them.

This need for radical but necessary change in the composition of the engineering team posed a big dilemma for senior management. The legacy engineering people had made significant contributions to the company's success, but their skills were no longer relevant. It would be a painful and distasteful decision to ask them to leave. Senior management would also have to ensure that the new people would have the necessary power to produce a Gizmo 2020. The action this company had to take is similar to what Steve Jobs did when he returned to Apple in 1997. He told Edgar Woolard, the lead board member at Apple and the former CEO of DuPont, that he would have to replace most of the engineers and bring in new designers who had the skills and power to move the company forward. The results speak for themselves.

Monitoring How the Nodes Are Working

Once you have defined your most critical decision nodes and who should be in them, consider how and how well they are working. Are decisions made both formally and informally? Does the person in charge of the node have the power, or is another person more influential? What information is being used—is it external, and is it used in real time? What decision rules are followed? You have to not only design the decision nodes properly, but also ensure that they have the right priorities and incentives, and probe or sample them often enough to know that they are working well and that the collaboration is happening. When they're not, you have to figure out why and make the fix. Maybe the decision maker has an organizational blockage, such as the inability to wrest the necessary expertise from another department, and the head of engineering refuses to free up the technical talent she oversees to participate in that node. Or maybe the person has a psychological blockage that prevents her from expanding her networks to get the outside perspective she needs. You may need to have serious discussions with those people. If you don't step in to keep the decision nodes in sync with external change and action, you are reinforcing rigidity.

Think of the necessary connections the node should have to sources of crucial information, expertise, and other decision makers. Good decisions require internal and external information that is continuously updated, and even the sources of that information might have to change. The common bias is toward internal information, with little time spent on the fast-changing externals. It is also toward familiar sources of information, usually in-house experts the decision maker has long-standing relationships with. Relying on knowledge that is strictly internal and removed from the action, combined with a tendency to think about what has worked in the past, creates a linear view of what lies ahead. The go-to sources of information might also be too homogeneous to create imaginative alternatives. Those limitations hamper steerability.

This is where digitization can be transformative. It gets information in real time and helps improve collaboration and decision making at the nodes, especially when connected to external sources. Just as new technology creates new possibilities for serving consumers, it also creates new possibilities for steering an organization. For example, an automotive company gets online digital data from several hundred geographical zones of its car sales in the United States. It then uses algorithms to dissect which brands in which geographies are doing well or not against competitors. As a result, the company is able to maneuver its promotional and advertising expenditures, and by using predictive tools, can determine how many units of what brands to produce in what plants.

An imaginative leader, whether born digital or not, will exploit the potential of digitization to leapfrog other companies that can't respond as fast. You could, for example, use big data and algorithms to feed information about consumer buying patterns directly to the decision nodes that need that information, so people can immediately make whatever adjustments they think are necessary—say, in product specification, product mix, or which sales channels should be given greater emphasis and advertising—as done by the auto company described above. Such direct connections increase speed.

Born digital companies like Amazon and Zappos build their edge not just by accumulating consumer data but also with the ability to act speedily on that information. Some decision making is automated with computers, but even when it isn't, there are few organizational layers for information to filter through. It gets to the decision makers instantaneously, and they can change priorities or direction quickly. Having had the use of decision technologies from their very beginnings, these organizations are streamlined, with information fed directly to the machines or the decision nodes that need it. Those possibilities are available to any company that focuses on the essential decision nodes and is willing to invest in new digital technologies.

You have to pay attention to whether power in the node is shifting. The organization's charts do not tell an accurate story about who has power, let alone how well they use it, because it is a static picture of people in key structures. You can trace power through who has influence and control of resources. Leaders who have been given formal authority over certain decisions might not be able to exercise it without the cooperation of those who control the resources they need. This is often where the wheels lock up and frustration builds.

A similar problem arises when the person in charge of the decision node has a lot of resources but won't allow those resources to shift. Left unaddressed, this type of rigidity is much worse at the top of the organization, where power is more concentrated. I have seen many great plans stymied by a higher-level person who won't allow her energetic subordinate to refocus, even when that person's expertise is needed elsewhere. An engineering manager who refuses to release engineers to work on a breakthrough project creates rigidity that thwarts the organization's ability to deal with uncertainty. Beware of other delaying tactics that cause rigidity in the decision nodes, including being unavailable for meetings; postponing decisions; incessantly asking for information and outside studies that are expensive and take a long time; not allocating money to new initiatives; and perhaps most insidious of all, the common trick of assigning a weak person to the initiative.

At the "Wraps & Caps Company," a major producer of packaging material for consumer products, "Mike Vitale," the head of innovation, controlled a huge budget. That fact was not explicitly considered when the CEO assigned an energetic young leader and team to develop new products for two markets the company was trying to enter. The team did their brainstorming and homework and proposed numerous ideas, but Vitale funded none of them. Resources went instead to product extensions in the company's existing markets. Worse, those projects were highly capital intensive, thus soaking up the cash that could have gone to new projects. The team was frustrated beyond belief, and for many months senior management wondered why the numbers weren't moving in the right direction. When the CEO finally got to the root of the problem, he put a new person in charge of innovation, one who maintained control of the company's innovation expenses but had different criteria for dispensing them. Wraps & Caps then started getting back on the rails.

Practically every organization has decision nodes that are interdependent with others, some of which may be outside the organization in the ecosystem. (Let's not lose sight of the fact that while I'm using the term *decision node*, these are real human beings who are interacting with each other and making decisions.) In large global companies, there are hundreds of nodes in a complex web of interdependency. A P&L manager for all of Brazil for a US-based multinational, for example, will be in charge of deciding the product mix, people selection, and resource allocation for the country, but will have to coordinate with the leaders who make decisions about product lines for the whole corporation at headquarters. The wrong one or two individuals with power can seriously damage the entire web of decision nodes. Steering becomes impossible, and the company is unable to act quickly enough.

Decision nodes are likely to go awry or become obsolete at some point, so be prepared to confront those issues promptly. As people act and react, you will discover new things, and the organization will have to adjust. Stay alert for when you need to step in and dissolve the blockages or redesign the decision nodes. Long & Short's Jenn Hedley created her JPSs only after she had identified the decisions that were crucial to the organization's success and how those decisions would have to be made differently. She later reshaped the composition of that node when the organization needed to make technology decisions that would affect ten different project silos.

As president and CEO of the Cleveland Clinic, Dr. Toby Cosgrove redesigned the decision nodes but subsequently had to figure out why they weren't working as well as he had hoped. That led him to change the leadership criteria. He had undertaken the change soon after he took the helm in 2004. He wanted to shift the central focus from departments of medicine to areas defined by a patient's problem, such as cardiovascular or neurological. His idea was to have all the caregivers whose work related to that ailment become part of a common organizational unit; for example, psychiatrists, neurologists, and neurosurgeons would all be housed in the same facility and work together. "We realized that medicine had gone from an individual sport, where you have the image of a doctor with his black bag making house calls, to one that is a team sport that involves a lot of people," he explains. "I remember being taught as a resident that we looked after the skin and its contents, and we didn't have to have any help. Now with the total amount of knowledge in health care doubling every two years, no one individual can manage all of the information, so it has to be team play."

Cosgrove was essentially creating new decision nodes in which information would be shared and decisions jointly made based on what was best for the patient. Then he had to decide who would lead those nodes, and in the first round, he says, "I made some mistakes. When I announced that we were going to do this, nobody said it was a terrible idea but everybody was incredibly anxious. They didn't know who they were going to report to, where their office was going to be, and so on. And I thought it was important for these new units, what we called institutes, to have national stars in the leadership roles.

"I started with the Neurologic Institute. I identified somebody from the West Coast who had a big resume, a huge number of publications and a lot of National Institutes of Health grants. But it just didn't work out. I found that we needed a different kind of leader in those jobs, people who were great collaborators and understood our culture, even if they didn't have the biggest academic credentials. That was a major shift for us about how we picked people to lead."

———

YOU CAN'T STEER an organization properly without making the necessary shifts in decision making. The same can be true of shifts in financial resources, the subject of the next chapter.

CHAPTER 15

Steering on Two Tracks

YOU MAY HAVE a creative and well-thought-out plan to go on the offense, but you will still have to sustain your existing business for some period of time. You can't allow it to fall apart just because you are trying to put a new one in place; it is the only thing you have to generate the cash you need to fund the future. Yet at the same time you have to shift decision making, bring in new expertise, and change people's priorities to the new initiative. This dual track creates enormous stresses, particularly among those at higher levels of the organization who are being adversely affected. People who sense that they're losing power will procrastinate, hide resources, distort the changes you need to make—usually hoping the new thing will go away. Their reactions may stir up your own self-doubt and test your leadership. You will have to become a master in managing the transition at the appropriate speed.

Setting Short-Term Milestones

Once you know where the organization must go and have explained that to others, define the specific steps that must be taken in the near term to move onto that new path. It's a matter of working from where you want to be backward to the present and identifying the steps that will move you along. These items become the short-term milestones of your new path that you must hit one, two, or three quarters out. They are the front end of your long-term goals.

For example, when Tata Consultancy Services set out to build a new business around helping customers go digital in early 2014, it had to build the right kind of talent base. Creating the new business was a longer-term proposition; recruiting expertise in software engineering, channel sales, and contract negotiations were interim steps. Seeta Hariharan, general manager and group head of the new unit, hired 235 people in seven months, including veterans of Microsoft, Red Hat, and Informatica.[18] Had she not moved on that item, the new business would have failed to meet expectations. It was an important short-term milestone on a longer journey.

Short-term milestones don't have to be quantitative. Examples of qualitative milestones are exploring opportunities in certain markets in order to decide among them and learning about a new technology to determine the best way to adopt it. But they must still be specific; you can't just paint a picture of where you want your organization to go and leave it at that. Even if you believe in empowerment and delegation and are inclined to trust other people, you have to translate your idea from fifty thousand feet to fifty feet to make it actionable.

Executing on those milestones doesn't mean you can ease up on operating intensity for the existing business; you must execute on both tracks. I have seen many people make major shifts in the business without losing operating discipline, largely because they recognized the connection between the two. Some of the best are in India, where successful leaders are accustomed to an environment of great constraints and unpredictability, yet see the opportunity for tremendous growth in their own and neighboring economies. Analjit Singh of Max India describes everyday business conditions this way:

> Margins in almost every business are under constant assault, the Indian government regulates pricing in some industries, costs of many inputs are rising, wage inflation is high, and consumer expectations are continually ratcheting up because of digitization. So there's margin pressure on just about anything you look at. And especially if you're a publicly listed company, where news airs every day on TV and everyone is running around looking for short term gains, strategic decisions get challenged. Trying to meet the demand of the hour constrains your ability to play out the strategy. Decisions get compromised because of the constant drum beat for another cent in earnings per share every day, week, quarter. How do you cope with it? By staying very very focused, and getting better and better at what you do. There is no room for marginal players.

Ivan Seidenberg, CEO of Verizon for seventeen years, was a master of this balancing act. He led the company through multiple transformations in telecommunications, a task that required meeting the demands of the marketplace Verizon was competing in while contending with the wishes of myriad government regulators (federal plus some twenty states). Each wave of mergers and acquisitions changed the competitive dynamics, gradually tilting the game to players who could provide the seamless connectivity and data intensity consumers demanded. From its roots as a "Baby Bell" called Nynex (one of the landline telephone companies the US government created when it broke the Bell Telephone monopoly into seven smaller regional companies), Verizon worked diligently to operate efficiently so it could keep its landline business robust and profitable as it simultaneously built a national wireless network.

Then in the 2000s, Seidenberg made a huge bet. The delivery of wireless and wireline telephony, TV signals, and Internet access had been in flux for years, creating a kaleidoscope of players, technologies, and customer bases that changed each time an acquisition or partnership was announced. Much to the chagrin of government regulators, who tend to see small as beautiful, waves of consolidation swept the industry, fueled by the economic reality of two forces: first, consumers' desire for seamless connectivity—in other words, no dropped cell phone calls whether you're calling out of state or in your home state—and ready availability of broadband access and content; and second, providers' drive for efficiencies of scale.

Verizon was already building the standard for high speed mobile networks. Seidenberg saw that consumers would want video and computer signals coming into their homes, and the copper wires that connected customers' landline telephones couldn't provide enough speed. So he set out to replace Verizon's copper network with fiber optics. The plan was hugely expensive—$23 billion over ten years—and controversial, because it was based on a view of how the technology, the regulatory framework, and consumer preferences would evolve at a time when all of those things were highly uncertain. At the time, cable wasn't a big threat to Verizon's current business, but as Seidenberg looked five years out, he could see that it would be.

Seidenberg describes the balancing act this way:

We had to have operational excellence to extend the current franchise, and we had to change the business model in light of our broader view of the external environment. It's the distinctive role of senior management to pull the levers to make that happen, to ask the right questions, allocate the resources in a way that allows *both* things to happen. The greatest companies find a way to have that mix. We spent maybe fifty percent of every day making sure the current business was working right, and maybe twenty-five percent thinking about whether the things we were currently doing would still work next week or next year or the year after that, because analysts and shareholders and boards usually take a one- to three-year view. Then the other twenty-five percent is spent on whatever you need to do to make sure that you're positioning yourself to be successful in the fourth, fifth and sixth year and beyond.

We weren't good at it at first, but as we got better and more systematic, our progress and performance were more level. We were getting great results from the current operations, achieving the milestones by extending our franchise, and as the things we had put in place two years earlier began to bear fruit, we feathered them in. So each year you're feathering in the payoff from something you acted on several years earlier.

Keeping the New Path in Focus

You need to track the short-term milestones of your new path just as intensely as you do costs, gross margins, and the like—and be just as swift to take remedial action when something deviates. You will likely have to create new metrics for them and monitor them on a dashboard separate from your short-term financial and operational goals. Then you have to ensure that you have the relevant information flowing to you, and the right people in the room, so you can assess progress at least once a quarter. If you don't create a separate review, you have to be fierce in protecting the time you allot to monitoring your milestones.

The milestones will show whether your new path is working and what course corrections are needed. For example, a legacy company that needs to build capability in software and algorithms must track progress vigilantly: Are the experts being hired? Are they being integrated into the important and appropriate decision nodes? Are they being listened to? You need intense personal discipline to follow up on these things and keen listening to discern signals that they are stalled. When Jenn Hedley of Long & Short picked up on the fact that the people in sales and marketing were not using the segmentation information the technology experts were generating, and the technology experts were not incorporating marketing expertise, she intervened, revisiting the issue every two weeks to make sure people were listening to each other.

Your first action steps will undoubtedly trigger reactions from other players, so you will face unsettled variables about how the external landscape will shift. Reviews will keep you informed about whether your assumptions are turning out to be correct and your path is still viable. Within the company, use rigorous reviews to sniff out friction in the social system caused by changes in decision-making power and the assignment of people. And you will need to stay attuned to the financial impact, particularly on the critical supply of cash, as you extract resources from one part of the business in favor of the new path. Digging to the root cause of the deviations will reveal what's getting in the way. It's common, for example, for people to be assigned to a growth project—even multiple ones—without being relieved from their usual tasks. Having too many projects in the works takes its toll, because people are stretched too thin. Even a company with a billion dollars in revenue can't successfully pursue more than ten game-changing innovation projects.

Your discipline in following through on both the existing trajectory and the short-term milestones of your new path is key to steering. Follow-through can take place in your existing budget and operating reviews, your JPSs, and conversations you initiate for this purpose. But it also includes actions you take as a result of what you learn. Falling short on either track diminishes your ability to steer. When you discover deviation, find the root causes. Don't jump to conclusions, but don't delay. Most root causes are internal, primarily issues with people who simply do not want to get on the new train.

Let the Numbers Flex

Budgets can be the strongest tool for steering onto the new path and making adjustments along the way—provided perceptual acuity and numbers regularly meet. As I have noted previously, however, budgeting is a stubborn core rigidity and therefore a huge constraint on steering—not just the actual budget, but how people perceive the process and what they think the boss will or won't do. In most companies the budget is a commitment, and with it come the goals that are the basis of performance evaluation and compensation. Bosses aren't necessarily interested in how the numbers were achieved, what might affect them in the future, or what external realities might impinge on them. In particular, the outside world must be part of the budgeting and review process, and the numbers must be allowed to change when circumstances change. The tighter the linkage between the numbers and the internal and external realities the company is facing, the better you'll be able to steer. Even Wall Street's lust for short-term results is no excuse for locking onto numbers for too long. Performance without steerability can shorten the life of the business. In any case, those investors don't care about how resources are allocated internally; they look at results for the corporation as a whole.

One effective technique for making those midcourse corrections is the rolling two-year budget, wherein you map out spending quarter by quarter for the next eight quarters. You revisit the budget each quarter, extending it to the next eight quarters each time, shifting resources based on whatever new information you have. A wireless telecom company, for example, might adjust the advertising budget if it sees its churn rate (the percentage of dropped subscribers compared with new ones) take a hit. Auto sales in the United States depend heavily on what the Federal Reserve does. Budgets will have to be adjusted at the first sign that such movement has begun. Why wait for the year to end?

Looking out two years while adjusting the budget every quarter gives you flexibility while providing a longer-term plan. At the end of the first quarter, you're looking out at the ninth quarter, so you are always scanning ahead, but you are also staying in tune with the current realities and the most up-to-date projections of where the business is going. That flexibility is enhanced when the new numbers reflect feedback about customers and shifts that might affect sales in upcoming quarters.

But you have to maintain discipline while making the organization steerable. A boss who withdraws resources or raises targets midstream without explanation creates a new layer of uncertainty for middle managers and raises suspicion about his motivation. Was something missed? Or is the boss trying to raise his own career stock by driving hard on the numbers before his next move? Changes in budgets and KPIs that force people to cut corners and borrow from the future are, at the end of the day, destructive to the social system and the company's longevity. "Neil," for example, was feeling pretty confident in his new job of sales manager when he answered the call from his boss in June 2013. Near the end of the third quarter of the fiscal year, he was well on his way to meeting the annual target. But the conversation felt more like a drive-by shooting than a pat on the back. The boss suddenly raised Neil's target by 50 percent, and it was clear that Neil might be out if he didn't reach it. Neil and I talked just a few days later, and he was still shaken. He had tried and failed to persuade his boss that the target was unattainable.

Neil got this sudden surprise because the boss had her own realities to contend with. Two of her direct reports had run into trouble and warned her that they would miss their numbers. The only way she could make up for the other misses was to get what was lacking from Neil's area, and she was not going to ease up, because she knew shareholders would accept nothing less. The boss had made her career by putting harsh demands on people, getting them to deliver at least in the short term, then moving on. Neil had a choice: do some high-pressure selling and deep discounting to deliver the numbers by October, or get ready to leave the company.

Neil's boss may have been right if she saw marketplace potential Neil didn't. But if that were the case, she failed to provide the clarity, dialogue, and coaching, as well as the link to external realities, that would have made the demand more palatable. A two-year rolling budget and frequent adjustments for external realities will reduce end-of-year surprises like this and keep the business on track.

Shifting resources in light of current realities happens naturally at some companies. At Google, for instance, the highly secretive Google X lab tries to invent solutions to some of the world's biggest challenges and create new core businesses in the process. To qualify as X-worthy, the solution must have the potential (echoing the founders' original mission statement) "to change the world." Google's deep pockets allow it to fund these long-term explorations and still deliver respectable earnings without a lot of pressure from shareholder activists seeking to disgorge some of that cash. Although the time horizon for new growth areas is long term, reviews are frequent and tough. The aim is as much to kill projects as it is to grow them. Killing the less promising projects frees up resources to focus on others. As Rich DeVaul, who heads the project evaluation process, says: "Why put off failing until tomorrow or next week if you can fail now?"[19] Yet when obstacles arise for a promising innovation, the course correction is immediate. Astro Teller, who directs day-to-day work at Google X, told *Fast Compa-ny*'s Jon Gertner that when more money was needed for one such project, CEO Sergey Brin and CFO Patrick Pichette had no hesitation in adjusting the resources to keep it on track: "Thanks for telling me as soon as you knew," Pichette said. "We'll make it work."[20]

At an officers' meeting of a $10 billion industrial company I attended in 2010 along with several board members, "Kim Lee," head of the medical device unit, made the usual twenty-five-minute presentation. Among other things, he identified several opportunities to expand, the most attractive being in northwest China. At the end, the CEO returned to the bullet point about China. "What would it take to build the business there?" "We would have to find the best distributors," Kim explained. "Why are we going through distributors?" the CEO continued. It would be faster, but yes, there were some negatives. The CEO asked about alternatives, one of which was to build their own sales force, and after some discussion of the pros and cons, that seemed like the clear winner. "But we don't have a big enough budget," Kim said. "Well," said the CEO, "Should we do something that is strategically incorrect because we don't have the budget for it?" He turned to the CFO and said: "Let's find the $5 million Kim needs." And they did, shifting budgets right then and there to attack the new growth market.

Unfortunately, this isn't the usual outcome when people propose initiatives that will require adjustments to the budget. I have seen only a few companies that do this kind of shifting. But it should become a common practice. It releases a ton of energy and reduces the game playing. Middle managers have to become flexible in accepting these adjustments. So does the CFO, who is critical to changing the psychology around budgets and KPIs. He or she is the trustee of all financial allocations. If the CFO is inflexible, locked into certain patterns for dispensing funds, and refuses to let the outside world filter in, go back to your understanding of decision nodes and consider whether the right person is at that node. A CFO who plays offense will find the funds needed for the new path, by either changing the internal allocations or discovering new sources of funds from outside, and will also be open to adjusting compensation.

Changes in priorities, budgets, and KPIs must go hand in hand. Over time, people will be conditioned not only to expect more frequent changes in these things, but also to bring their own sense of realism to the table. In 2013 "Mariana," the leader of a consumer goods division in Brazil, had a solid plan to take the business from $1 billion to $1.4 billion worldwide in three years. She was confident that she would win support from her bosses. But when she presented the plan, the reaction was lukewarm. "It's not aggressive enough," the senior team said. "This is a very profitable business. Why can't you get it to $1.4 billion sooner? If you don't see a way to achieve that, we'll retain consultants to help you."

Mariana had spent her life in this business. If there were a way to accelerate growth, surely she would have seen it. Still, she had little choice but to see what the consultants had in mind for meeting the target. She conducted interviews and chose one of the world's best firms to analyze the business. The research was extensive and deep, probing the company's standing with customers as well as quantitative data. It confirmed her view, ultimately showing that while some product lines were very profitable, others were lousy, and some were barely making money. The $1.4 billion target was achievable three years out, but the best way to strengthen the business was to do some judicious pruning and redirect the resources to grow the remaining lines. Revenue growth would be suppressed in the short term, but she would indeed hit the $1.4 billion target with a time delay of a few years.

So Mariana was convinced she was on the right path, but that didn't mean the bosses would accept the proposition. How would she persuade them? As she ran the imaginary conversations through her mind trying to anticipate every question and reaction, she realized that if the bosses didn't accept the delay, she would probably have to leave the company. Was she really prepared for that? She also knew that missing the revenue target meant that she would miss her bonus, which represented a big portion of her total compensation.

The dilemma put her in a psychological funk for weeks, but finally she hardened her resolve. She would do her best to justify her plan to the higher ups, and if she had to miss her bonus, so be it. If they simply couldn't accept the lower number and asked her to leave, it would be their loss. With that, the matter was settled. In a matter of days, she presented her revised plan.

Mariana brought realism to the numbers, but her senior managers couldn't accept it. She had picked up subtle cues from the CFO of her division, who had been talking to the CFO at headquarters, but now the message was loud and clear: "Don't push back." Mariana was subsequently fired. Her bosses hired a replacement, and guess what they did next: lowered the targets.

If you expect middle managers and people on the front line to be the eyes and ears that pick up early warning signals, budget sessions and reviews should invite their input and suggestions for change, and especially their sense of realism. That doesn't mean making excuses or easing up. Playing footsie with the numbers to improve one's personal standing should be grounds for firing. We know for sure that most companies have made ethics and safety part of their culture. If you violate the principles around ethics and corruption, you're out. The message is reinforced by making a public show of violations and communicating it repetitively. Industrial companies now repeat the message about safety at every meeting; those who violate it get punished. You need to create an environment in which people are keenly attuned to the external environment and are willing to suggest changes when budgets and KPIs are causing rigidity.

Financial Resilience to Withstand Shocks and Transitions

As you move onto your new path you will have to redirect cash, take on more borrowing, sell some assets, or find a partner to fund the investment. Steerability increases when you build the capacity to withstand a shock if something unexpected strikes the business or to quickly muster the resources to attack when the opportunity is right. You obviously do not want to divest, spin off, or wind down the existing business when it's your cash generator. Maintaining liquidity while building a new venture that is not yet generating cash requires vigilant management. The foundation for financial resilience consists of two main sources: financial strength and relationships. Financial strength—capital structure, working capital, and cash generation and usage—must be managed with uncertainty in mind. That means taking advantage of leverage, but also weighing how much borrowing capacity to preserve for unexpected events and opportunities. You don't want to be forced to sell the crown jewels if an unexpected shock occurs. You might have some less productive assets that could be sold to raise capital, but you don't want to unload them at rock bottom prices. In India, for example, several infrastructure companies borrowed heavily to keep pace with the country's fevered economic growth between 2000 and 2008. When interest rates started climbing beginning around 2010, and the central government's paralysis limited the availability of coal and gas, some of those players ran into liquidity problems and had to sell off assets.

Managing working capital in uncertain times requires discipline to be sure that accounts receivable don't get stretched so far out that you can't collect, or you lose liquidity. Customers are also subject to uncertainties that could constrain their ability to pay. Inventory is riskier when uncertainty is high, because the probability of obsolescence increases. Cash is clearly an advantage when clouds gather, because you can use it to make acquisitions that bring technical expertise, footholds in a new market, or technologies, and to make the transition. Google's sizable cash reserves have allowed it to pursue ambitious long-term growth projects and acquire companies that give it a foothold in important new technology areas. Microsoft's cache allowed it to pounce on Nokia, a key part of migrating away from its dependence on software to the exclusion of devices.

Excessive cash, of course, can be a magnet for suitors and a certain kind of shareholder activist. You can guard against this by making sure that you have clarity about the new path for the business and its use of cash and take pains to communicate the reality. Apple came under pressure in 2013 from shareholder activist Carl Icahn, who thought the company should distribute much of its sizable hoard to shareholders. He began buying shares in August, increasing his stake to $3 billion by January 2014. The company had already announced a plan to return some money to shareholders in the form of dividends and share buybacks, but Icahn pressed for more. Other shareholders, however, maintained their faith in management's ability to use the capital wisely, including CalPERS and New York City's comptroller. So did Institutional Shareholder Services, the firm that advises shareholders and champions their rights. Icahn gradually lowered his demands; Apple CEO Tim Cook scaled down the buybacks and dividends and was able to make some investments for the future. In fact he went on a bit of a buying spree, acquiring more than a dozen companies in 2013 and the first half of 2014.

"AllReady," a leading distributor of industrial supplies such as maintenance and repair equipment, based in the Southeast, had a healthy business churning out profits and cash. Then the threat of digitization emerged on the horizon. Just as one retail sector after another had been damaged by the likes of Amazon and eBay, business-to-business suppliers too started to become vulnerable to online channels. All-Ready had a loyal customer base and extensive warehouses and distribution facilities that had long been a competitive strength. Now, however, those fixed assets could put it at a disadvantage against a prospective digital player. The management team had to figure out what its new path might be, and importantly, how to manage the transition without creating a loss of confidence among investors.

The senior team saw that they needed to give their customers more buying options by becoming omni-channel. They would have to move fast to build a digital presence, and it would be expensive. Fortunately, AllReady had the financial resilience to make a bold move. Its balance sheet was strong, especially its debt to total capital ratio, and it was generating lots of cash. The CEO set out to recruit the expertise the company needed, set up a separate division, and stood up to insiders who protested the increased attention and resources that were being channeled to the new division—one that would have low margins and would take a long time to mature. Absent the financial strength to fund the new plan, the thriving company would have made itself vulnerable to being overtaken.

Financial resilience is not just a matter of piling up cash. It includes resources that might be available to you because of the reputation you've earned and the relationships you've established. Sunil Bharti Mittal was against the wall in 2013 when his company got squeezed by thinning margins and rising interest rates. What pulled him through was not a stash of money; the company didn't have enough, and it was heavily in debt. Rather, it was his reputation as a disciplined operator and builder of businesses that took the company through a tough time and helped prepare it for the next phase.

Mittal is the founder and chairman of Bharti Enterprises, the parent company of Bharti Airtel, a global telecom giant based in New Delhi. With business savvy and intense operational discipline, Mittal had grown the company from a small start-up fighting for a share of the brand new mobile phone market in New Delhi to the largest mobile phone company in India. It was a tough fight all the way. In the early days, he used partnerships to scale up quickly, then later came up with a new business model, whereby partners built the networks and ran the back office information systems. That arrangement freed up time and money for Bharti to build its wireless franchises even faster. In 2010, driving for scale on a global basis, the company expanded into twenty-three African countries in one fell swoop by buying the African mobile phone assets of Zain Group. Investors were impressed by Mittal's prowess. At the time he announced his intention to make the Zain acquisition, the phone was ringing off the hook with bankers offering to lend the money.

Then around 2011 the team discovered that the infrastructure in many of the African countries was less developed than they had thought, and that lots of cash would be needed to refurbish the acquisition, while competitors were waging fierce price wars in the local markets. The formula of attracting customers at entry prices and eventually selling higher-margin services didn't work well in much of Africa, so revenue growth was slower than planned. Meanwhile, barriers to entry in India fell due to regulatory changes, and price wars broke out on the domestic front as well. Interest rates and inflation were rising in India, the rupee lost value, and the company struggled to service its debt. Cash became painfully tight.

Determined to right the ship, Mittal identified some assets that could be sold or spun off. He reached out to some investment bankers who respected his business acumen and reliability, and they helped the company get the financing it needed to get through the rough spot and on to its next phase. Since then, the competitive winds have changed, prices have started coming back up, and the financial picture is improving. Mittal's reputation and relationships proved to be as valuable as cash in dealing with the uncertainties that beset the company.

Keep Others with You

As you transition, keep feelers out to know how various constituencies are reacting. Since by definition you're veering from the existing path to something untested, good people can have different judgments and confidence levels. People who are not in your camp might see the transition as an opportunity to dislodge you.

CEOs have to be especially concerned about investors and their boards. Pressure to deliver short-term results emanates mostly from a vocal segment of the investment community that trades the stock. Comparisons are made against forecasts that management previously announced, or against a consensus among security analysts or performance of a peer group. In many cases, missing forecast earnings per share even by a penny on a base of $2.50 is considered catastrophic and sends the stock price into gyrations. The pressure cascades down from the board and the executive suite to the lowest levels of the organization.

The majority of investors are not, however, short-term traders; some 70 percent of the stock of publicly traded companies is held by institutional investors, who tend to keep it in their portfolios for more than a year. When they are dissatisfied, they move in a block. If you earn credibility with them, they may buy more. As the leadership teams at Google, Apple, and Amazon have clearly shown, you can keep investors with you if you explain the path you're on and deliver on the interim steps. Meeting the short-term milestones on the longer-term path you have defined will increase your credibility.

Bringing the board along is essential, but it can be tricky. Often a single director can undermine the CEO's plan. You have to know where the internal power lies and keep information flowing so such differences of opinion do not come as a surprise. Sharing information to help the board see what you see will help you win the board as a partner. "Tru Posture," a manufacturer of ultra-high-end office chairs and other furniture sold to architectural firms and office equipment suppliers, is one of many companies at the critical juncture between the old and the new—and with a board that straddles both worlds. With about 10 percent market share and $2 billion in annual revenue, the company is profitable, and despite slowly declining overall demand, its traditional business has considerable room to grow by gaining market share. Its customers and users agree that it makes superlative products.

What's changing is that the millennial generation is entering the office space. They work long hours, are health conscious, and expect that even a mundane, seemingly slow-changing product such as an office chair should make use of digital tools to make a great product even greater. The company saw a chance to go on the offense. It started a pilot program to develop a technology-driven ergonomic chair that uses sensors in the back, seat, and arms to send information about the user herself—her pulse, heartbeat, stress level, and posture—to her smart phone. The customer can then make adjustments in the chair to enhance comfort and alignment of the spine—and, hopefully, raise her productivity.

It took TP a year and a substantial investment to make and test the prototype. Now the company has to make the commitment to scale it up, which means hiring expensive technology experts and building the necessary digital infrastructure. This will require a huge cash investment, which is largely expensed and thus will lower earnings per share in the short run. Investors won't be pleased. Existing suppliers can't provide much of what will be needed, so TP has to find new ones; those long-term relationships could be strained. All of this has to take place without solid knowledge of how the market will respond and whether a born digital company will radically alter the industry. Perhaps the most difficult problem is the people: making the change from those who helped make the company successful over many years but whose skills are no longer as relevant. Once the company sets off in its new direction, everyone will know that the existing business is going to be diminished. The best talent might leave.

All of these issues are weighing on not only the senior team but also the board, which is divided. A long-tenured, highly influential board member believes that the company should expand its existing business, since it has the capabilities and brand and knows little about this new business. "We know our core business," he said, "and there's room to grow. We know nothing about playing this new digital game." But another board member, a high-level executive at a born digital company, has seen companies like his completely reshape whole industries. Why wouldn't digital technology disrupt this business as well, he wondered, and why should TP be a laggard? The board continues to be divided as of this writing, leaving the CEO hanging and concerned about the precious time that is being lost.

As we saw in the previous chapter, Verizon CEO Ivan Seidenberg proposed in 2004 a massively expensive plan to build out a fiber optic cable network that would carry Internet, cable, and voice signals across the United States. He and his team were convinced that the expenditure was essential to Verizon's future, but they had to win over at least one important constituency: the board of directors. Seidenberg didn't use his team's presentations as a sales pitch. He had a close working relationship with his directors and regularly shared information about current shifts in the external environment. Meeting after meeting, he updated them about regulatory changes, what competitors were doing, and new developments in technology. He brought in outside experts to talk about the technology and its future capabilities, and manufacturers to talk about what they saw coming.

The board dug deeply into the issues and constantly tested management's plan, but it confirmed what he saw and fully backed him, even when analysts criticized the bold decision. Seidenberg kept the dialogue going, and investors eventually came around to see the wisdom of that judgment. Only now is AT&T following suit.

The essence of keeping people with you is communication: of the facts, of your point of view about the things that are not yet clear, and of the likely second- and third-order consequences. If you have done all this and convinced no one, you may want to rethink your plan. That doesn't mean you have to back off, though. Ultimately, leadership is not a vote. You lead by your convictions. As Seidenberg says, "There comes a day when you have to say 'This is what I believe.' If the investment in fiber optic cable didn't work, the board probably would have changed management. I was fine with that."

IN THE NEXT CHAPTER we will see how one leader and his team responded when their business was hit with a barrage of bruising surprises.

CHAPTER 16

Merck's Quick Organizational Turn to Offense

YOU ARE GOING to face skepticism, if not outright resistance, as you navigate your business through uncertainty. You need a resilient inner core, a deep-rooted belief that you can overcome whatever obstacles arise, and intensity in executing on both your short- and long-term goals. You also need to be attuned to people's need for clarity about a common sense of purpose and to the practical issues that arouse people's fears, such as career goals and compensation. Responding to a sudden change, resetting the path quickly, and steering the organization with a steady hand might seem like a tall order, but that is the challenge you must be prepared to face, as Jay Galeota did as president of the Hospital & Specialty Care business at Merck in late 2012.

As Galeota's leadership team revisited their projections for the current year and longer five-year horizon, they were deeply concerned by what they saw: a slowdown in their compound annual growth rate and a significant miss on operating profit. Tracking the performance of other pharmaceutical companies and assessing their pipelines are routine at Merck; gauging the timing and uptake of competing drugs is part of that routine. But as the year evolved, the "knowns" had suddenly changed, and many new uncertainties were manifesting in a way that was negatively impacting the business. Galeota and his leadership team were put to the test: Could they turn quickly from defense to offense, act fast to reset the path, and steer the organization onto it?

Galeota had become president of the Hospital & Specialty Care business when Merck created it in 2011 to better serve the unique customer sets of its specialty businesses. The group included the global commercial franchises for Acute Care Hospital, HIV, HCV, Neurology & Immunology, Oncology, and Ophthalmics, which combined were generating roughly $10 billion in revenue, representing more than one in every five dollars Merck made. The group had its own research and manufacturing functions, which worked closely with those functions at the corporate level.

In that first year Galeota drove typical cost containment actions and began to break down the value of each of the businesses within his group to better understand its individual contribution to his organization and to Merck overall. In planning for 2013, there were good reasons to expect that revenue growth for Hospital & Specialty Care would continue for the near term. With strong brand management, increased scrutiny of expenses, and targeted investments, the team could handle some bumps in the market. They worked hard to build a realistic and achievable set of objectives in several major treatment areas, such as HCV and HIV. They knew that competitors were working on alternative treatments, and they also knew how the regulatory environment worked. Their base case planning scenario was that none of those alternative treatments would get FDA approval for at least another year or two. This view of the competitive landscape, coupled with the current performance trends, was the basis for the strong business performance Galeota and his team built into their five-year plan. Where there were internal skeptics, it was because they thought the growth and profitability goals were too modest. For example, one of Merck's drugs for treating brain cancer was going off patent soon, but some felt strongly that doctors would be reluctant to accept a generic substitute for such a serious condition. Meanwhile, new drugs in Hospital & Specialty Care were working their way through Merck's pipeline, promising to make up for any near-term declines in existing product performance, and many believed these would come to market as planned.

When the team met in early 2013 for their operations review and to assess the dynamics of the market landscape, several new developments started to emerge. The first was in the area of hepatitis C. Competitor Gilead's new oral treatment hadn't even cleared regulatory hurdles when it dealt a huge blow to Merck's market leadership. The market took a rapid and dramatic shift to warehousing patients. This is a phenomenon in which doctors put their patients' treatment plans on hold when they anticipate that a better therapy is coming soon. Many patients with hepatitis C don't exhibit symptoms for years. For those asymptomatic patients, doctors felt comfortable forgoing existing treatments, even those that were very good, in favor of something that promised greater benefits, such as being easier to take or requiring a shorter course of treatment.

Merck was in the midst of launching a new, injectable hepatitis C treatment (Victrelis), which was expected to contribute substantial growth for the Hospital & Specialty Care business. However, with the unexpected early promise of Gilead's oral treatment, the market contracted to a fraction of what had been projected. This had serious and immediate implications for Merck and for other competitors in the current HCV treatment market. A multibillion-dollar market for the newly launched treatments nearly disappeared.

As if that weren't enough, Merck also faced an intensifying competitive environment in the treatment of HIV due to new FDA regulatory guidance for accelerated or "breakthrough therapies." The FDA has long had a "fast track" approval process to speed the approval of treatments where a medical need is not being met. In late 2013, Congress passed a law that introduced an even faster process for treatments designated as "breakthrough." This designation is for drugs that promise to be a significant advance in treating serious or life-threatening conditions. The FDA works creatively with the sponsoring company and dedicates resources to shepherding these therapies through the review process. As a result, two new treatments for HIV, one from Gilead and one from ViiV (an independent company combining expertise from GlaxoSmithKline, Pfizer, and Shionogi), received that designation and came to market very quickly. While leaders at Merck knew that competition was coming and had plans to handle the new dynamic, they were focused on a different time frame. This accelerated competitive environment for the HIV market, compounded by the massive shift in the HCV market, put significant pressure (about $3 billion worth) on the group's revenue and even more pressure on its operating profits.

Other uncertainties also emerged. One significant change was a regulatory shift in Europe that brought generic competition to Merck's immunology business sooner than expected. Biosimilar products, which historically had not been approved in Europe, were back on the table. Regulators usually did not allow data to be extrapolated from one molecule to another—meaning that even a slight variation in any part of the development candidate would require separate testing. But the European regulators unexpectedly took a different tack, allowing drug developers to extrapolate data from one use of the drug to another, known as bioequivalence. This seemingly small change from a regulatory point of view opened the door to wider use of competitors' products and a much clearer path forward for biosimilars, creating a serious threat to a double-digit growth area in Merck's Hospital & Specialty Care business.

Yet another uncertainty that went against expectations was physician behavior in the area of oncology. Merck's patent for Temodar, a brain cancer drug, expired, and a generic version was released. The group had planned for that, but it wasn't clear how quickly physicians would switch to a generic substitute for such a serious condition. As it turned out, they shifted sooner than expected, and that market too experienced accelerated erosion.

Galeota summed up the impact of these four developments and the imperative to rethink the business: "It became clear to us that the growth we had in our business plan would now be significantly lower than what we needed it to be over the five-year plan. We needed to figure out what to do to fill that gap quickly."

The Big Revelation

What do you do when your growth projection is far below where you want it? One option is to hunker down, cut costs, and prepare for the negative fallout. Another is to expand your view and harden your resolve to find new opportunities to grow. As the new realities came into sharper focus, Galeota went on the offense. He pulled together a team of six high-potential, innovative leaders from a mix of areas across the company to take a critical look at his business—and the outside world—to figure out where the opportunities were and, just as important, where they were not. He selected a senior sponsor from his leadership team and handpicked a high potential team member to lead the entire effort from start to finish. Each of the team members would work with the franchise lead, the project leader, his or her respective direct reports, the markets, and the needed support functions to assess the state of the total business and propose a path forward.

All the different businesses Hospital & Specialty Care competed in had long been viewed as equally important. At budget time, the conventional practice had been that the leaders who made the most compelling case for resources for their line of business got the lion's share. Galeota knew it was time to step back and rethink that approach: "Every business franchise aggressively pursued growth and argued hard for the resources to do so. They thought they were supposed to, and the incentives worked that way. But I began to see that we needed to understand our P&L better. Which businesses threw off the greatest return, had the greatest expectations for growth, and could therefore lift operating performance? Which were less profitable and stagnant? Might there be a different way to participate in those, or a way to exit? The thought was that by making clearer choices, our performance would improve."

Thinking more precisely about which businesses could create value and which would drag performance became a joint project for the core group of leaders Galeota picked to support this effort. Working closely with Galeota's direct reports, this project team put their heads together to sort the businesses into three groups with labels that suggested what they would actually do with those businesses: Invest to Win, Participate in a New Way, and Monetize. Proper sorting depended on an accurate view of how the market context affected the growth prospects of each of those businesses, coupled with the internal strength and stability of the business and prospects in the pipeline. To better understand that context, the team worked closely with the key regions and markets to incorporate their knowledge and perspectives. In addition, the team used internal market data and secondary information sources to imagine what the future might look like for each business.

One key set of observations had to do with the challenges facing hospitals around the world. In all global markets, whether in China or the United States or Japan, hospitals were a fast-evolving nexus of care, and they were all trying to reduce their costs while recognizing that they needed to evolve in order to better control outcomes and prevent costly readmissions. As the team homed in on that part of the healthcare delivery chain, a hypothesis emerged: acute care was an underappreciated growth opportunity. The business already served hospitals with treatments for various conditions, but this insight pointed to something different. Instead of defining the company's efforts by the disease it would tackle, as the division had always done, it could focus on hospitals as a customer segment or channel and probe their needs more broadly. Merck then would pursue ways to make things better for those customers.

Then the analytics went into overdrive as the team ran through the set of test questions they had constructed at the outset. Did hospitals represent a big area of unmet medical need? Affirmative. Was the customer segment sustainable? Yes. Did Merck have a strong base to compete in this newly defined segment? It did. Was the competitive environment appropriate for investment? It was. Was there tractable innovation in the space? Yes. The idea of focusing on the broader needs of hospitals passed through all the screens. The segment was attractive and worthy of disproportionate investment, and Merck could uniquely compete in it.

"From there we put a lot of precision around sorting areas of unmet need that were the highest drivers of direct and indirect cost for hospitals to see how we matched up," Galeota explains. "For example, we saw significant cost burdens for institutions managing patients with hospital-acquired bacterial infections—an average cost of $108,000 per patient. We had new antibiotic programs in our pipeline, plus we had new formulations of existing products in our plan, so that was a good fit. Several other areas of high unmet need and high cost burden to hospitals were identified, and while we didn't have immediate treatments available, we had the global infrastructure in place to deliver products to the customer if we could find them outside our company. In other words, we could bias our product line toward areas of unmet needs and high costs for hospitals in order to find ways to fill these gaps and better serve our customers. That was a moment of revelation."

What about competitors? There was no clear leader. Most of the big pharmaceuticals were not investing in the market that Merck was now rethinking. This was understandable, because the regulatory framework and payer landscape were just beginning to come together around addressing the unmet need and lack of incentive for development in this segment. Formal research was consistent with the new idea; hospitals were saying that if Merck went ahead and brought innovative products to areas of unmet need, they would be very interested, especially where no big advances were on the horizon. Even payers and government regulators were aligned, because they too had an interest in advancing treatments in problem areas like fungal infection and infectious disease.

Swimming Downstream

All the external and macro trends were telling the team that their hypothesis about the hospital segment as a growth opportunity was correct—they were swimming with the current, as Galeota put it. But they were underinvested in that space, which posed both strategic and organizational challenges. The question became what they could do differently to grow that segment and how to do it.

The team decided on four "pillars of growth." The first was to leverage their existing products through increased promotion and more precise targeting, and also to extend the science around them by encouraging more investigative grants and research. The second was to accelerate drugs already in the pipeline, where patients often had no other alternatives. One way to accomplish that was to be proactive with the FDA, to show, for example, that treatment for infection was not unlike treating cancer: a patient comes to the hospital and acquires an infection, then suffers a prolonged isolated experience in the intensive care unit, usually with a negative outcome, and at a high cost to the health-care system and a high burden to the patient, the family, and the care providers. The FDA took a similar view. It put a new antibiotic that was in Merck's pipeline on an accelerated track, which would allow it to get to market much sooner and at lower cost, provided it performed as expected.

The third pillar was to aggressively seek other companies that had products that could help address hospitals' areas of highest cost and unmet need and where Merck didn't have anything in development. And the fourth pillar was to give hospital customers support beyond therapeutic intervention. Specifically, there were data supporting the fact that the time taken to identify an infection, the particular "bug" causing the infection, the appropriate treatment, and the administration of the first dose all had a huge effect on a patient's outcome. Patients who were treated faster were far less likely to become critical. So Merck put together a program called "Antimicrobial Stewardship," showing that protocols and communication standards helped hospitals cut the time between the initial diagnosis and the first dose of the correct medication.

The runway ahead was energizing, but there was a catch: limited resources. "We had a fixed amount of resources like everyone else in the industry," Galeota explains, "so we had to liberate funding to realize this opportunity in serving hospitals." He and his team took a careful look at each of the other businesses—oncology, HIV, immunology, hepatitis, neurology, and ophthalmology—and ranked them along the same parameters that showed hospitals to be a potential "win." This included five-year compound annual growth rates, contribution margins, and pipeline valuations. Some were strong, and some were clearly in the "monetize" category. Immunology, HIV, and HCV were in the middle and received more rigorous assessment. They became candidates for focused investment. For the businesses that didn't measure up, the team looked to see if they could exist profitably outside of Merck. The team's hypothesis was that these businesses would be worth more to Merck externally than internally compared with other opportunities in house.

At that time, oncology was a question mark. Early data on a new kind of cancer drug called an anti-PD1 inhibitor, which activates the body's own immune system to attack the tumor, looked remarkably promising. Merck might have been on the cusp of a major breakthrough. But the findings were not yet conclusive, so it was too soon to declare oncology a winning area. So the team recommended a clear decision rule: if the science came through, go all in and create a separate business unit; if not, exit the business. In subsequent months, anti-PD1 inhibitors did prove to have high potential for Merck, and the company took the team's recommendation to move oncology into its own business unit. This new class of drugs could become one of the most meaningful advances in cancer treatment in thirty years.

Sharing the Pain and Gain

By the end of the first quarter of 2013, with the economic, analytical, outside-in, customer-driven exercise behind them, it was time for the team to shift into execution mode. At many companies, this is when passive-aggressive foot-dragging and pushback from senior leaders often subvert the best laid plans. Merck didn't experience that; focusing on the people side, including the right stakeholders in the strategy development and being clear on interim targets, proved to be a winning formula. Once senior leadership approved the plan to reshape the business, Galeota took a couple of key people from the project team and asked them to spearhead implementation.

The greatest impact of Hospital & Specialty Care's new direction was on people—some of the very leaders who had helped define the new path along with another ten or so managers across the division could be personally affected. Some of their businesses were going to decrease in size; some would be spun out altogether. Yet if the team didn't pull together to negotiate the bend in the road, the whole organization could go off the rails. Exiting ophthalmology, Parkinson's disease, and schizophrenia, for example, was part of the plan that would enable the other businesses to grow through reallocation of resources.

Two years earlier, the team had created a set of "operating principles" for managing the businesses within Hospital & Specialty Care and how they were going to do it. The key to these principles was that they tasked the leadership team to look at the business as an enterprise, not merely as a collection of individual businesses. One key principle was to assume positive intent—that is, to assume that team members were doing all they could to improve the broader organization. Team members kept the principles front and center in fun ways, such as pop quizzes at meetings and recognition

for those who showed they were exemplifying the intent behind these principles.

As the team moved into implementation mode, these
principles proved to be vitally important. Galeota says, "We
knew we were asking people to do things that were uncon-
ventional at Merck and uncomfortable for them. It had
always been the case that if you put a smart business case
together, it would get supported. Suddenly we were saying
that it wasn't your job to see how many more dollars you
could get. It was how effective you were at creating the efficiencies we needed in order to redirect resources to the
most profitable growth areas. This was a huge change, and
we knew it would be hard. We took the human side of this
very seriously."

The incentives supported that perspective. "We told people that if they were committed to this new direction, they
and the organization would be in a better position coming
out," Galeota says. "They would be placed in a different and
ideally better role somewhere else. But people also understood that if they were unable or unwilling to make the shift,
they would be replaced. Taking a holistic view of talent actually allowed us to upgrade talent in key areas at the same
time."

The commitment from those who stepped up was impressive, Galeota notes, including from some of the leaders
who were working themselves out of a job. "Even people in
areas that were no longer a priority going forward felt liberated by the clarity of the plan. Choices around resource
prioritization, expense reduction, and risk became a lot easier once this clarity was declared," he explains. "Managers
knew not to bring forward business development ideas that

weren't in our areas of focus or that didn't meet higher hurdle rates around risk or return. They knew where they were expected to spend their time and energy."

To drive the change, the team used a simple but rigorous tracking process: a two-page dashboard of key elements of the plan, including steps toward divesting ophthalmology and neurology assets, assessing partnership opportunities, and enabling the four pillars of growth in the hospital area, which they revisited every two weeks. Clear accountability and frequent monitoring of progress against interim goals kept them maniacally focused on execution from April to November 2013.

By November, as the team started to put its profit plan together for the following year, they ran the pro formas five years out to see where they stood relative to their initial growth aspirations. They were tracking a little ahead of where they wanted to be for 2014 and within just 2 percent of the target five years out, despite additional challenges that came to the market. This was no small feat, as the new plan was built on an aspirational goal of 20 percent improvement over baseline projected five-year compound annual growth rate. The refocusing returned the group to growth despite the hits to hepatitis C and HIV; and the divestitures of the US ophthalmic and schizophrenia businesses went as planned, supporting the team's hypothesis that these businesses were worth more to Merck outside of the company. By early 2014 the newly designed core business was gaining momentum, growth was up, expenses were down, and morale was positive. Consistent with the initial recommendations, the implementation plan shifted to focus on truly driving investment in Acute Care Hospital, which was showing strong signs of robust growth, as the team had hoped it would.

Pinpointing New Uncertainties

Uncertainty has not been completely eliminated, but Hospital & Specialty Care now feels better prepared to deal with it. "Our ability to define market segments accurately is not our greatest uncertainty," Galeota says, "nor is the changing science in the hospital space or the regulatory environment. Competitors had changed the environment to their advantage and surprised us, but we recognized the pattern and learned how to facilitate the environment to our advantage."

"Our greatest uncertainty now is execution," Galeota adds. "We had to make significant choices to make the organization stronger, which took courage to execute. One of the best outcomes from the work has been the renewed dedication of the leadership team to demonstrate a state of constant dissatisfaction with the status quo. Bringing the entire leadership team together around implementation even on aspects not directly related to their own businesses has created an environment where the team can question and challenge choices in the spirit of maximizing growth opportunities and continually work to optimize our approach to the business."

The net result is that Merck is on the alert, steerable, and vigilant in executing on two tracks. "It's a personal challenge for me to stay focused on and true to the vision while continuing to bring others along," says Galeota. "Then it's a matter of discipline to stay on track with what we need to do in the short term to achieve our goals further out. We have to stay on top of the internal and external realities. It's a daily battle, but one worth fighting."

CHECKLIST FOR PART IV

✓ How agile and steerable is your organization relative to the speed of external change?

✓ How would you implement a JPS in your unit? What blockages do you anticipate?

✓ Have you explicitly designed the decision nodes in your organization? Do those nodes have the right kinds of expertise, the right resources, and the right leadership to move with speed?

✓ How often do you monitor and diagnose the most important decision nodes? Do you take remedial action, including changing the leader, promptly when needed?

✓ Are you willing to extract resources and people from parts of the organization that are becoming less important to the company's future? Do you shift resources to adequately fund new business opportunities?

✓ Do you have clear short-term milestones to make progress on your longer-term path? How well do you balance your focus and resources between the current business and the activities and investments that will build the future?

✓ When you see new opportunities, do you engage your colleagues, direct reports, and bosses to help them see what you see, especially the external context that makes your idea compelling to consumers? If you are a CEO, do you frequently discuss the external context and new opportunities with your board?

✓ Are you building the financial resilience to withstand structural uncertainty and pounce on opportunities?

A FINAL WORD

CONTINUALLY STIMULATING YOUR thinking and self-reflection is a critical aspect of building and maintaining your attacker's advantage. To be successful in this era of structural uncertainty, you need the following five capabilities. Rate where you are on each of these on a scale of 1 to 10 (10 being the highest), then consider how you will improve. You might also consider doing a 360 on yourself using these criteria.

1. Perceptual acuity
2. A mind-set to see opportunity in uncertainty
3. The ability to see a new path forward and commit to it
4. Adeptness in managing the transition to the new path
5. Skill in making the organization steerable and agile

You will find a comprehensive checklist at ram-charan.com.

ACKNOWLEDGMENTS

||||||||||||||||||||||||||||||||||||||||||||||||||||||||||||||||||||||||||||||||||||||||||||||||||||||||||||||||||||||||||||||||||||||||||||||||||||||||||||||||||||||||||

This book began when a client in India asked me to advise him on how his organization could deal with uncertainty. I can't say that the request surprised me; the Indian government alone is a source of great uncertainty for business leaders. But it did challenge me. In my quest to find practical solutions, I met and worked with a number of brilliant leaders, whose wisdom is reflected in the content of this book. I am very grateful for their insights and their willingness to share with readers some of the most enlightened leadership practices on the planet. These people include Anish Batlaw, Vic Bhagat, Kishore Biyani, Steve Bolze, Larry Bossidy, Bruce Broussard, Kris Canekeratne, Richard Carrión, Subhash Chandra, Bill Conaty, Dr. Toby Cosgrove, Mark Cross, Howard Elias, Maria Luisa Ferré, Mark Fields, Larry Fink, Todd Fisker, John Flannery, Jay Galeota, Deb Giffen, Kiran Kumar Grandhi, Hugh Grant, Raj Gupta, George Halvorson, Ron Heifitz, Chad Holliday, Tim Huval, Jeff Immelt, Sanjay Kapoor, Brian Kelley, Muhtar Kent, Jack Krol, Vinod Kumar, Terry Laughlin, Bill Leaver, Vinod Mahanta, Brian Moynihan, Alan Mulally, Kathleen Murphy, Arun Narayanan, Rod O'Neal, Tony Palmer, Raj Rajgopal, G. M. Rao, John Rice, Steve Schwarzman, Ivan Seidenberg, Deven Sharma, Analjit Singh, Dean Stamoulis, Charles Tribbett, Joe Tucci, Jørgen Vig Knudstorp, Brian Walker, Alberto Weisser, Jack Welch, and Major General Larry Wyche.

John Mahaney, my editor at PublicAffairs, applied his unsurpassed expertise in ensuring the best possible experience for readers. He dedicated an enormous amount of time and mental energy to bringing this book to fruition. I am very grateful for his substantive and editorial inputs.

I also wish to thank the senior team at PublicAffairs, namely, Clive Priddle and Susan Weinberg, who were tremendous supporters and critical advisors and to publicity director Jaime Leifer, publicity manager Chris Juby, marketing director Lisa Kaufman, and associate marketing director Lindsay Fradkoff for their skillful work in bringing this book into a complex and changing marketplace. Collin Tracy did a superb job in managing all aspects of the book's production and Sharon Langworthy did a thorough and wonderful copyediting of the manuscript.

For the past twenty years Geri Willigan has been my collaborator in helping me develop content and working with me as writer, editor, researcher and project manager. Geri has, once again, made indispensable substantive and editorial contributions to this book, applying her keen analytic mind to a tremendous amount of information and helping shape both the conceptual framework and presentation of material.

Charlie Burck, a former senior editor at *Fortune* magazine, lent his probing intellect and superb writing skills to this book. He has the rare capability to dig deep into a complex subject and then communicate it in a way that is easy to grasp.

I also want to thank my longtime business associate, John Joyce, who provided useful feedback at several critical junctures.

Researching this book involved scores if not hundreds of trips to far-flung parts of the world. Cynthia Burr and Carol Davis are the magicians in my Dallas office who kept me moving and on track. They are the infrastructure that allows me to traverse the globe and still function on a daily basis. I greatly appreciate their value-added.

NOTES

1. Andrew Edgecliffe-Johnson, "Online Courses Open Doors for Teenagers," *FT.com*, March 26, 2013, http://www.ft.com/intl/cms/s/0 /c5a4b932-924c-11e2-851f-00144feabdc0.html#axzz2UdebusFD.

2. Negative working capital is a combination of inventory and accounts receivable so low that they are much less than accounts payable; the more the company grows, the more cash it generates.

3. Ken Auletta, *Media Man* (New York: W. W. Norton, 2004).

4. http://www.automotivehalloffame.org/inductee/hal-sperlich/789/.

5. Krithika Krishnamurthy, "India to Be Launch Pad for Amazon's Plan to Deliver Packages Using Drones; Deliveries May Start by Diwali," *Economic Times*, August 20, 2014.

6. Jeff Bezos, Julia Kirby, and Thomas A. Stewart, "Institutional Yes: The HBR Interview with Jeff Bezos," *Harvard Business Review*, October 1, 2007.

7. A "customer" is the individual or company that purchases a good or service; a "consumer" or "end user" is the individual or company that actually uses it. Barnes&Noble is a customer for book publishers; the reader is the consumer or end user.

8. "Digital Leadership: An Interview with Jack Levis, Director of Process Management at UPS," *Digital Transformation Review* [CapGemini Consulting], January 5, 2014.

9. Shelly Banjo and Drew Fitzgerald, "Stores Confront New World of Reduced Shopper Traffic," *Wall Street Journal*, January 15, 2014.

10. This example is based on two Harvard Business School cases: Anette Mikes and Dominique Hamel, "The LEGO Group: Envisioning Risks in Asia (A)" (January 24, 2014, case no. 9-113-054), and Anette Mikes and Amram Migdal, "The LEGO Group: Envisioning Risks in Asia (B)" (December 10, 2013, case no. 9-114-048).

11. I have borrowed the term "steerability" from an insightful chapter by Hock-Beng Chea and Henk W. Volberda, "A New Perspective of Entrepreneurship: A Dialectic Process of Transformation within the En-

trepreneurial Mode, Types of Flexibility and Organizational Form," in *Entrepreneurship and Business Development*, ed. H. Klandt (Aldershot, UK: Avebury, 1990), 261–286.

12. "Decluttering the Company," *The Economist*, August 2, 2014, 53.

13. "Leading in the 21st Century: An Interview with Ford's Alan Mulally," *Insights & Publications* [McKinsey &Co.] (November 2013).

14. Michael Distefano and Gill Kurtzman, "The Man Who Saved Ford," *Briefings* [Korn Ferry Institute] (Fall 2014).

15. Ibid.

16. Bryce G. Hoffman, *American Icon* (New York, Crown Business, 2012), 102.

17. The notion of decision nodes was inspired by Nobel Laureate Herbert Simon's thesis on the anatomy of decision making. See also his book *Administrative Behavior* (New York: Free Press, 1949).

18. Chris Murphy, "Can Digital Business Make Tata a Software Company?" *Information Week*, February 14, 2014.

19. Jon Gertner, "The Truth About Google X: An Exclusive Look Behind the Secretive Labs' Closed Doors," *Fast Company*, April 15, 2014.

20. Ibid.

INDEX

RAM CHARAN is a world-renowned advisor to CEOs, business unit managers, and boards of directors who value his practical solutions to complex business problems. Dr. Charan earned MBA and doctorate degrees from Harvard Business School, where he graduated with high distinction, and is the author (with Larry Bossidy) of the international bestseller, *Execution: The Discipline of Getting Things Done* and many other books.

PublicAffairs is a publishing house founded in 1997. It is a tribute to the standards, values, and flair of three persons who have served as mentors to countless reporters, writers, editors, and book people of all kinds, including me.

I. F. STONE, proprietor of *I. F. Stone's Weekly*, combined a commitment to the First Amendment with entrepreneurial zeal and reporting skill and became one of the great independent journalists in American history. At the age of eighty, Izzy published *The Trial of Socrates*, which was a national bestseller. He wrote the book after he taught himself ancient Greek.

BENJAMIN C. BRADLEE was for nearly thirty years the charismatic editorial leader of *The Washington Post*. It was Ben who gave the *Post* the range and courage to pursue such historic issues as Watergate. He supported his reporters with a tenacity that made them fearless and it is no accident that so many became authors of influential, best-selling books.

ROBERT L. BERNSTEIN, the chief executive of Random House for more than a quarter century, guided one of the nation's premier publishing houses. Bob was personally responsible for many books of political dissent and argument that challenged tyranny around the globe. He is also the founder and longtime chair of Human Rights Watch, one of the most respected human rights organizations in the world.

. . .

For fifty years, the banner of Public Affairs Press was carried by its owner Morris B. Schnapper, who published Gandhi, Nasser, Toynbee, Truman, and about 1,500 other authors. In 1983, Schnapper was described by *The Washington Post* as "a redoubtable gadfly." His legacy will endure in the books to come.

Peter Osnos, *Founder and Editor-at-Large*